CONNECTING HISTORY

Germany

1815–1939

Euan M. Duncan

Boost

HODDER
GIBSON
AN HACHETTE UK COMPANY

Every effort has been made to trace all copyright holders, but if any have been inadvertently overlooked, the Publishers will be pleased to make the necessary arrangements at the first opportunity.

Although every effort has been made to ensure that website addresses are correct at time of going to press, Hodder Education cannot be held responsible for the content of any website mentioned in this book. It is sometimes possible to find a relocated web page by typing in the address of the home page for a website in the URL window of your browser.

Hachette UK's policy is to use papers that are natural, renewable and recyclable products and made from wood grown in well-managed forests and other controlled sources. The logging and manufacturing processes are expected to conform to the environmental regulations of the country of origin.

Orders: please contact Hachette UK Distribution, Hely Hutchinson Centre, Milton Road, Didcot, Oxfordshire, OX11 7HH. Telephone: +44 (0)1235 827827. Email education@hachette.co.uk. Lines are open from 9 a.m. to 5 p.m., Monday to Friday. You can also order through our website: www.hoddereducation.co.uk. If you have queries or questions that aren't about an order, you can contact us at hoddergibson@hodder.co.uk

© Euan M. Duncan 2022
First published in 2022 by
Hodder Gibson, an imprint of Hodder Education,
An Hachette UK Company
50 Frederick Street
Edinburgh EH2 1EX

www.hoddereducation.co.uk

Impression number   5   4   3   2   1
Year   2026 2025 2024 2023 2022

Cover photo © INTERFOTO/TopFoto
Illustrations by Integra Software Services Pvt. Ltd., Pondicherry, India
Typeset by Integra Software Services Pvt. Ltd., Pondicherry, India
Produced by DZS Grafik, Printed in Bosnia & Herzegovina

A catalogue record for this title is available from the British Library.

ISBN: 978 1 3983 4533 1

SCOTLAND EXCEL

We are an approved supplier on the Scotland Excel framework.

Schools can find us on their procurement system as: **Hodder & Stoughton Limited t/a Hodder Gibson.**

Contents

Welcome to Connecting History!

The aim of this series is to provide rich and accessible information that will help learners, teachers and lecturers to get the most out of History. The series has dedicated resources for National 4/National 5 and Higher History. It sparks interest, provides the right level of detailed information and is straightforward to access through its consistent and clear structure.

Overall, Connecting History is designed to provide a fresh approach to the study of History. The series is:

- **Consistent.** The content of each book is structured in a similar way around the key themes of the course. This clear structure will make it easy to find what you need when studying History. Indeed, all books in the series are designed this way, so that every book, for every unit, is equally accessible. This will make it quick and easy to find the information that learners and teachers need, whether revising, extending study or planning a lesson.
- **Focused.** Up-to-date course specifications have been used to create these books. This means that it is easy for learners and teachers to find information and provides assurance that the books offer complete coverage of the examinations, as well as general study. This means that you will not have to read through multiple long texts to collate information for one content area – our authors have done this already.
- **Relevant.** The importance and significance of each area to your understanding of our world and history has been clearly set out. Background sections in each chapter capture issues in their entirety, and sub-sections go into detail on key issues, with a number of sources and interpretations included. These texts go beyond the standard material that has been in circulation for a while and bring in new opinions, evidence and historical scholarship to enrich the study of History. We hope that this will continue to foster not only an ability to be highly successful in History, but also to inspire a love of the subject.
- **For today.** These units are not just about the past, they are about today. Themes of social justice, equality, change and power are all discussed. The most up-to-date research has been reflected by our authors, old interpretations have been challenged and we have taken a fresh look at the importance of each unit. We firmly believe that it is impossible to understand the present without a firm understanding of the past.
- **For tomorrow.** This series prepares learners for the future. It provides the knowledge, understanding and skills needed to be highly successful in History exams. Perhaps just as importantly, these books help learners to be critical and curious in their engagement with History. They challenge readers to go beyond the most obvious or traditional narratives and get to the bottom of the meaning and importance of the past. These skills will make readers not only successful learners, but also effective and responsible citizens going forward.

We hope that you enjoy using the Connecting History series and that it fosters a love of History, as well as exam success.

Several units in this series are supported by digital resources for planning, revision, extension and assessment in Boost, our online learning platform. These will be updated annually to reflect recent course and assessment updates. If the nature of the assessment changes, or the skills are tweaked, fear not, our digital resources will be updated to reflect this. To find out more about this series – including the Boost resources and eBooks – visit **www.hoddergibson.co.uk/connecting-history**

Our academic reviewers

Every Connecting History textbook has been reviewed by a member of our Academic Review Panel. This panel, co-ordinated by our Academic Advisory Board, consists of nine Academic Editors with links to the University of Glasgow across a range of historical specialisms.

Each Academic Editor reviewed our texts to ensure that the:

- historiography is in line with the latest research and scholarship
- content is culturally appropriate, up to date and inclusive
- material is accurate and states facts clearly.

This book was reviewed by Professor Ray Stokes, Chair of Business History and Director of the Centre for Business History in Scotland at the University of Glasgow. He teaches courses in German history and comparative history of business and technology. He has published widely in these areas, including co-authoring *Building on Air: The International Industrial Gases Industry, 1886–2006* (Cambridge University Press, 2016).

Academic Review Panel	Units reviewed
Professor Dauvit Broun, Professor of Scottish History	Higher: The Wars of Independence, 1249–1328 National 4 & 5: The Wars of Independence, 1286–1328
Dr Rosemary Elliot, Senior Lecturer (Economic & Social History)	Higher: The Impact of the Great War, 1914–1928 National 4 & 5: The Era of the Great War, 1900–1928
Dr Shantel George, Lecturer (History)	National 4 & 5: The Atlantic Slave Trade, 1770–1807
Dr Ewan Gibbs, Lecturer in Global Inequalities (Economic & Social History)	Higher: Britain, 1851–1951
Dr Lizanne Henderson, Senior Lecturer in History (Interdisciplinary Studies)	Higher: Migration and Empire, 1830–1939 National 4 & 5: Migration and Empire, 1830–1939
Dr Mark McLay, Lecturer in American History	Higher: USA, 1918–1968 National 4 & 5: Free at last? Civil Rights in the USA, 1918–1968
Dr Alexander Marshall, Senior Lecturer (History)	Higher: Russia, 1881–1921 National 4 & 5: Red Flag: Lenin and the Russian Revolution, 1894–1921
Professor Ray Stokes, Chair of Business History (Economic & Social History)	Higher: Germany, 1815–1939
Dr Danielle Willard-Kyle, Research Associate	National 4 & 5: Hitler and Nazi Germany, 1919–1939

Academic Advisory Board	Dr Karin Bowie, Senior Lecturer in Scottish History, University of Glasgow
	Dr Philip Tonner, Lecturer in Education (History), University of Glasgow

Introduction

The country we now call 'Germany' went through tremendous change during the nineteenth and twentieth centuries.

In 1815, Germany did not exist as a united country and unification of the German states seemed a long way off. Romantic ideas of a German 'nation' had been growing in popularity, and intellectuals advanced the ideas of one German *Volk* (people) who deserved their own political home, a united Germany.

Yet, the unification of Germany was a relatively slow process. Although during the revolutions of 1848 it appeared that the German states might have been close to uniting under one parliament, this did not come to pass. The regional particularism of the German states acted as a barrier to growing nationalism, as did the interventions of neighbouring Austria. Indeed, it was not until Prussia came to dominate German affairs, and grew strong enough to resist the influence of Austria and the reluctant German states, that unification was made possible.

This united Germany grew in strength and power. It was this Germany that entered the First World War in 1914. Though enjoying some military success, particularly in the early years of the war, Germany was ultimately defeated. Germany's last-ditch attempt to defeat the Allies on the Western Front failed, and in 1918 it was forced to surrender.

The impact of the war was felt keenly in Germany. Kaiser Wilhelm II abdicated and fled to the Netherlands. A new government was formed, although it was soon faced with numerous challenges and crises. Economic depression, unemployment, hyperinflation, and political assassinations and instability plagued the early years of the new Weimar government. The government survived these challenges, entering a 'Golden Age' in 1924. However, this stability would not last. By 1929, economic problems were once again plaguing Germany, and the 'old guard' of civil servants, military personnel and business leaders turned away from Weimar. So too did those middle-class and older Germans who viewed the economic crisis of the late 1920s and early 1930s as the fault of democracy. Governments came and went with alarming regularity, and support for pro-republic parties waned.

It was in this political and economic crisis that support for Hitler and the Nazis soared. Hitler was unpopular with the aristocratic elite in Germany, but was eventually offered the role of chancellor after President Hindenburg feared the Nazis would disrupt parliament and prevent recovery. Hitler acted decisively and, by 1934, was secure in his position as the supreme leader of Germany.

The Germany Hitler created was exclusionist, violent and repressive. He was able to control the nation effectively from 1933 to 1939, as will be discussed in the last chapter.

This book covers all of these areas in greater detail, and will allow you to gather the knowledge and skills needed to write strong essays for this unit.

Good luck!

Chapter 1

An evaluation of the reasons for the growth of nationalism in Germany, 1815–50

The aim of this chapter is to evaluate the causes of the growth of nationalism in Germany between 1815 and 1850.

LINK TO EXAM

Higher

Key issue 1: this chapter will examine the factors that led to the growth of nationalism in Germany, allowing pupils to judge the main reason or reasons why it grew.

Background

In 1815, Germany as we know it today did not exist. Rather than a single, unified state, a collection of separate, small kingdoms coexisted around the borders of modern-day Germany. These states, including, among others, Bavaria, Franconia, Saxony, Swabia and Thuringia, had been part of the so-called Holy Roman Empire. Though not especially united, this collection of states did, at times, have a significant role to play in the politics of central and southern Europe. By 1789 around 22 million Germans were living in 314 states. Over a thousand towns had near full **autonomy**, and each region had its own rulers, traditions, laws and **sovereignty**.

This empire had a permanent imperial **Diet**, and each of the states sent representatives to attend proceedings. The Diet was chaired by the **Habsburg** emperor. However, there was no central political power, no common system of taxation, no legal obligation for states to follow decrees and no **standing army**. In fact, in many ways this Diet nurtured the so-called **particularism** of the German states.

1

Germany lacked clearly defined borders, and the Holy Roman Empire included people who identified as French, Dutch, Danish, Polish and Czech, to name but a few. It was not only ethnically and linguistically varied but also divided religiously: the north was predominantly Protestant and the south mostly Catholic.

German development lagged behind Britain and western Europe. Development was slowed by the feudal system, common in most states, with large rural populations tied to the land they worked and the emerging middle class precluded from positions of political power. There was no universal currency or system of money, and a powerful **aristocracy** wanted to maintain this **status quo**.

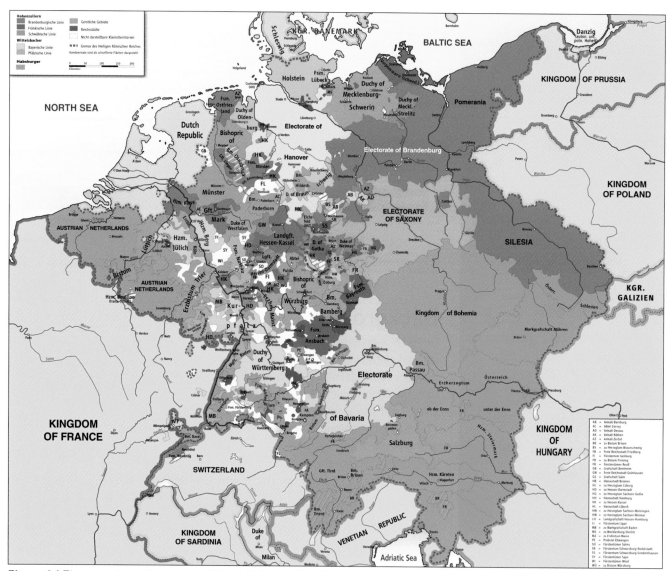

Figure 1.1 The map shows the nature of the Holy Roman Empire in the late eighteenth century. Note how many small states exist within the borders of what is now Germany. Also note the dominant position of both Prussia and Austria. Both played an important role in relation to the growth of nationalism in Germany

However, by 1815 the geopolitical situation in Europe had changed dramatically. The French Revolution and Napoleonic Wars had reshaped Europe, and in many ways had ushered in a modern age. Napoleon's defeat in Russia in 1812 and then at Waterloo in 1815 ended the French emperor's designs in continental Europe, but the changes the French Revolution brought left a lasting mark on the German states.

The German historians T. Nipperdey and D. Nolan highlight the importance of Napoleon in Germany in Source 1:

> **SOURCE 1**
>
> In the beginning was Napoleon. His influence upon the history of the German people, their lives and experiences was overwhelming at a time when the initial foundations of a modern German state were being laid. The destiny of a nation is its politics, and those politics were Napoleon's – the politics of war and conquest, of exploitation and repression, of imperialism and reform.
>
> **Nipperdey, T. and Nolan, D. (1996)** *Germany from Napoleon to Bismarck: 1800–1866,* **Princeton University Press**

By 1815, the Holy Roman Empire had been abolished and the number of German states had reduced to 39, a grouping known as the German Confederation. This body had one **executive**, or central authority – the Bundestag – presided over by Austria. Austria was deeply conservative and opposed both change and the emerging nationalism seen in Germany. Prussia, also very conservative, was emerging as the dominant power among the German states. Yet despite these conservative influences there is evidence of a growing nationalism within Germany between 1815 and 1850.

This chapter will discuss what historians call the **Vormärz** period, broadly occurring between 1815 and 1850. In many ways this was a period of oppression and suppression in Germany, with powerful rulers determined to maintain the political status quo. Yet it was also a time when a growing number of Germans began calling for a more united Germany. We will also examine the factors that led to this growth in nationalism.

1.1 What caused German nationalism to grow?

For the purposes of the examination, it is important to be able to evaluate the factors that caused nationalism to grow in Germany. This chapter sets out the main causes for the growth of nationalism and supports you in evaluating their relative importance.

This section will examine the following factors:

Economic factors
Cultural factors
Military weakness
Effects of the French Revolution and Napoleonic Wars
Role of the liberals

Understanding these issues will allow you to make a judgement on the main cause(s) of the growth of German nationalism between 1815 and 1850.

1.1.1 Economic factors

Although Austria was the dominant *political* force among the German states, Prussia was quickly becoming the dominant *economic* force.

When Napoleon was defeated, a peace treaty was drawn up at the Congress of Vienna, which was held from September 1814 to June 1815. The two states that benefited most from this settlement were Austria and Prussia.

Some historians argue that a desire among German states to cooperate economically created a situation where there was a greater willingness to cooperate politically, causing the growth of nationalist support.

Prussian economic development

After a series of catastrophic military defeats to the French, Prussia introduced a number of reforms. The reforms prompted widespread compulsory education and abolished taxes, tariffs and **serfdom**, which led to the growth of urban towns and cities. These modernisations allowed for significant economic development in Prussia in the years leading up to 1815, and the state grew in importance after the Vienna peace settlement was concluded.

In the peace settlement, Prussia made significant territorial gains in western Germany, including the rich states of Rhineland and Westphalia. Although Prussia was reluctant to take on these lands, instead preferring to consolidate power in the east, it acquired important economic strength as a result of the expansion. Its population doubled to nearly 10 million and it gained access to valuable raw materials.

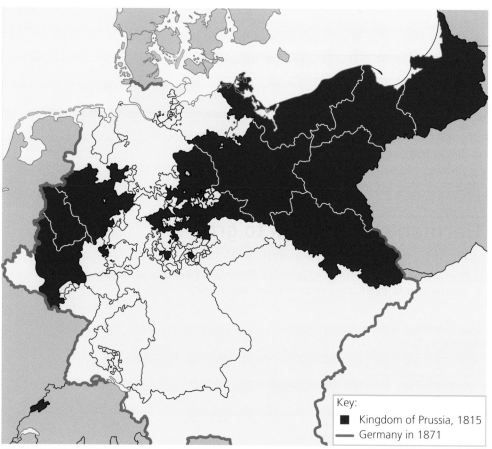

Key:
■ Kingdom of Prussia, 1815
— Germany in 1871

Figure 1.2 Prussia's population doubled in size as a result of the 1815 peace settlement, leading to it (somewhat reluctantly) being drawn into German politics

The historian M. Fulbrook points out the importance of this development in Source 2.

CONNECTING HISTORY: HIGHER GERMANY, 1815–1939

SOURCE 2

In the process [of expansion], it doubled Prussia's population and gave the previously economically rather backward state the benefit of mineral riches and areas more advanced in commerce and industry … The effective moving of Prussia westwards further shifted the balance of power between Prussia and Austria in favour of the former.

Fulbrook, M. (2019) *A Concise History of Germany* **(3rd edn), Cambridge University Press**

As Prussia became more economically powerful, it was drawn ever deeper into German affairs. With the new territories in the west, Prussia was poised to outstrip Austria in terms of economic development, which would come to play a critical role in the Industrial Revolution. This facilitated stronger German cooperation without the intervention of Austria. Therefore, Prussia's economic development can be said to be connected to the growing sense of German nationalism.

The Zollverein

After 1815, the 39 German states that had been created following the Congress of Vienna each used a different currency, and different weights and measures. Each state had its own economic policy and acted independently from all others. However, this changed during the Vormärz period.

Changes originated in Prussia. With increasingly spread-out lands following the territorial amendments in 1815, manufacturers in Rhineland complained to the Prussian king about the additional **customs duties** they were forced to pay. The expense was made worse by having to cross through multiple states, as Prussian lands were no longer **contiguous**. The king responded by introducing the Prussian Tariff Reform Law in 1818, which created a customs union that prevented internal tax on the movement of goods. The reform had an immediate economic impact and the Prussian finance minister, Friedrich von Motz, strove to expand the customs union beyond the state. While other customs unions existed in south and central Germany, the Prussian model was by far the most successful.

In 1834, Bavaria and Württemberg joined, and the newly enlarged union, the Zollverein, was formed. It was made up of 18 states and 23 million people. By 1836, this had grown to 25 states and 26 million people. By 1844, only Hanover, Mecklenburg, Oldenburg, some Hanseatic towns and Austria were not members. Austria preferred to form a customs union within its own empire, and so was excluded from the economic boom that occurred in Germany. The Prussian currency, the thaler, was adopted by all members of the Zollverein, leading Germany to become significantly more economically united.

Figure 1.3 A Prussian thaler from 1766, which by 1844 became the common currency for all member states of the Zollverein. With a single currency and no internal customs barriers, member states' economies grew rapidly

This economic integration had political implications for the growth of nationalism. The historian M. Fulbrook argues that 'moves towards economic unification presaged the form which political unification would eventually take'. The economic success which resulted from such cooperation led many Germans to realise the possibilities of a more united Germany. Economically, the states had proved their collective power – what could be achieved if they also cooperated politically? The idea led to growing nationalist fervour, particularly among liberals and the industrial middle class. Furthermore, the exclusion of Austria distanced the anti-nationalist Austrians from the economic progress within Germany, further contributing to the weakening of Austria and the rise in German nationalism.

The development of transport infrastructure

Along with increased economic cooperation and **industrialisation** came important developments in communications. Throughout the 1830s in particular the German states saw extensive roadbuilding programmes, the introduction of steam ships on large rivers such as the Rhine, an extension of the canal network and, crucially, the building of railways. Important lines, such as that linking Leipzig to Dresden in 1839, stimulated increased production, particularly of coal and iron. The greatest expansion happened in the 1840s with 1100 km of track being laid in 1846 alone. This promoted the growth of factories, like the Borsig Works, an extensive iron foundry in Berlin producing locomotives, and, while the majority of Germans still worked in rural areas, these changes laid the foundation for Germany's future industrialisation. The growing infrastructure made goods cheaper to transport, encouraged economic growth and created industrial demand.

Figure 1.4 The Borsig Works specialised in producing locomotives for the growing German rail network

The developing rail network contributed to the growth in German nationalism as it not only demonstrated the advantages that could be gained through cooperation but also allowed for the spread of ideas. German states became increasingly interconnected through road and rail, which helped break down regional barriers and local particularism, both of which had been a major impediment to nationalist growth. Nationalist pamphlets and papers could travel far and wide on the growing communication network, causing a further increase in the spread of nationalist ideas.

On the other hand…

Although Prussia was gaining in economic power and increasingly able to challenge the power of Austria, it remained a deeply conservative state. Prussia did not gain a united parliament, King Frederick William III dropped many modernising reforms and many reformers had been dismissed by 1820.

Moreover, the administration of the Zollverein did not always run smoothly. Any member of the group was able to propose or veto a proposal, meaning progress in some areas was limited.

Both points limit the strength of the argument that an economically dominant Prussia led to a growth in nationalism.

Overall

The Zollverein and growing Prussian economic dominance were clearly very important and contributed to an increasingly united and interconnected Germany. Indeed, the historian W. Carr called the Zollverein the 'mighty lever' of German unification.

1.1.2 Cultural factors

It was not only economics that caused a growth in German nationalism but cultural factors too. Partly, nationalism can be said to have grown out of emerging German literature which centred on the concept of the German **Volk**, those with a shared language and history. The **Romantic movement** also inspired many university students to promote the idea of German nationalism, and to think of Germany as the 'Vaterland' (Fatherland). Additionally, while France was growing more dominant, the German people were keen to establish a united front.

Language and culture

Some of the emerging elements of German nationalism prior to the French Revolution were set out by the German jurist, state journalist and politician Friedrich Karl von Moser (Source 3).

> **SOURCE 3**
>
> We are one people with one name and one language. We live under a common leader, under one set of laws that determine our constitution, rights, and duties, and we are bound together by a common and great interest in freedom … yet we remain the prey of our neighbours, the subject of their mockery, disunited among ourselves, enfeebled by our divisions, strong enough to hurt ourselves, powerless to save ourselves…
>
> **Moser, F. K. von (1765)** *Von dem deutschen Nationalgeist*, **Schaefer**

This dramatic extract encapsulates much of Moser's writing; namely, that Germans should be united by their language (*Sprachnation*), culture (*Kulturnation*) and community of remembrance (*Erinnerungsgemeinschaft*). He opposed the particularism of states, emphasising the commonality in Germans across the different states. He argued that Germans should be proud of 'their own' (*sein Eigenes*), which he emphasised in relation to a shared idea about what it meant to be German.

During the Vormärz period, scholar Heinrich Heine built upon Moser's ideas via his dispatches from Berlin, which also became highly popular in the context of developing nationalism. German philosophers such as Johann Fichte, Georg Hegel and Johann Herder developed this idea that Germans were a unique, **primordial** Volk and should all belong to the same state. Hegel argued that Germans had kept their language since ancient times, and this was used by some as a justification for growing nationalism and calls for a united Germany. Fichte, who became the most effective proponent of German nationalism, argued that Germans should be influenced by their supposed roots in northern Europe, rather than by France or the Catholic south. These philosophical arguments were made more popular and accessible through collections such as *Children's and Household Tales* (1812) by the Brothers Grimm, which contained over 200 folk tales that drew on Germans' common history and folk traditions. Through their writing, popular German authors also helped instil a sense of shared history and heritage, and blamed powerful neighbours, especially France, for the decline of German greatness.

The spread of these cultural ideals gave the German people a definition of what it meant to be German, providing justification for the creation of a united German **nation-state**. Importantly, this developed the sense of a shared identity, 'natural' characteristics and qualities, helping break down barriers between those from different states and encouraging a growing patriotism.

Universities and student movements

Much of this nationalistic philosophical thought was put into practice through the formation of student societies, clubs and national festivals. The German historian C. Jansen describes these groups in Source 4.

SOURCE 4

Until 1867, the prototype of a nationalist organization in Germany was not a political party, but publicly operating clubs and societies, with the national festival becoming one of the most significant expressions of organized nationalism … Organized nationalism appealed to intellectuals and the portion of the student body that created fraternities (Burschenschaften), the first explicitly nationalist organizations.

Jansen, C. (2015) 'The Formation of German Nationalism, 1740–1850', in H. W. Smith (ed.) *The Oxford Handbook of Modern German History*, **Oxford University Press**

Student fraternities, or **Burschenschaften**, began joining with **crypto-nationalist** gymnastic groups and calling for a strong, unified Germany that could stand up to its powerful neighbours, such as France. The General Association of German Fraternities was formed in 1818, made up of around 4000 students from 14 German universities. By this time, the gymnastic organisations had swelled to around 12,000 members. These groups organised and attended large festivals that called for the unification of Germany, for example in 1817 when a large number of organised nationalists from all regions gathered for a festival at the Wartburg Castle at Eisenach to openly oppose the existing political system and burn books that were critical of their movement. Similar scenes were seen at the Hambach Festival in 1832, where attendees called for a united, **republican** Germany. Around 25,000 to 30,000 people attended Hambach, although there was little consensus among them on how to achieve unification.

This led to a growth in nationalism as it gave students and intellectuals, who had been inspired by the ideas of the Romantic movement and philosophical discussions of nationalism, a way to express and advance their desires for a united Germany. In turn, this helped transform these ideas into real-world calls for political nationalism and unity.

On the other hand…

Austria was deeply concerned about this growing nationalist expression in Germany, and acted decisively to halt its growth. The Austrian chancellor, Klemens von Metternich, decided to clamp down on what he viewed as the dangerous growth of nationalism. The German parliament, the Bund, enacted the Carlsbad Decrees in 1819. These called for strict censorship, a ban on gymnastic societies and student fraternities, the suspension of radical lecturers and broad press censorship. This brought an end to organised nationalism after only a couple of years, suggesting that nationalist expression through cultural factors may be limited as a reason for increasing nationalism, since its growth was physically limited by Austrian conservatism.

Overall

It is clear that there was a great deal of Romantic and philosophical support for the idea of a German nation-state. Calls for a 'Fatherland' for all Germans stirred powerful, emotional demands for a united Germany, particularly among students, thinkers and writers. The fact that these Romantic ideas were given political voice through student fraternities also contributed to the growth in nationalism.

Yet, this also sparked opposition from Austria, arguably limiting the ability for these sentiments to develop further. Moreover, some historians, such as G. Mann, argue that these lofty theories were only ever consumed by a small elite, and that most ordinary Germans 'did not look up from the plough'. This suggests that cultural factors were perhaps not central to the growth of nationalism in Germany.

1.1.3 Military weakness

The military events of the late eighteenth and early nineteenth centuries revealed that a disunited Germany was militarily weak. Even the larger German states like Prussia were unable to fend off the military ambitions of neighbouring powers. Defeat left Germany vulnerable. Some historians argue that many Germans believed the unification of Germany would reverse this, which in turn led to the growth in nationalism between 1815 and 1850.

Prussian military weakness

While it was clear that Prussia was developing into the most important state economically, that was not true militarily. The immediate events leading up to the creation of the German Confederation had revealed the weakness of the Prussian military.

Although Prussia had been excluded from the Confederation of the Rhine, the precursor to the German Confederation, it was one of the largest and most powerful German states. However, in 1806, the king of Prussia, Frederick William III, unwisely decided to declare war on France. It became immediately obvious that the Prussian army was ill-disciplined and ill-prepared, with outdated tactics and equipment. This was amply demonstrated at the Battle of Jena, where Prussian forces were quickly and easily defeated by the French. The subsequent Peace of Tilsit saw Prussia lose significant amounts of land, in both the east and west. It was also forced to pay huge reparations for war damages and to accept that Prussian men would be forcibly enlisted in the French army.

Figure 1.5 Napoleon pictured at the Battle of Jena, on 14 October 1806. While the Prussian army was significantly larger than that of the French, Napoleon's tactical skill and modern army delivered a decisive defeat, with nearly four times as many Prussian casualties as French

It was becoming increasingly clear that a disunited Germany was weak and vulnerable to the machinations of neighbouring powers, especially in relation to French power – the German people particularly resented the forced conscription of 119,000 Germans into the French army in 1808. Nationalism grew, as many Germans felt the only way to resist the impositions of more powerful (and united) countries, and to guarantee German security, was to form a united nation with a powerful army.

German weakness

The political structure of Germany in 1815 was based on the German Confederation, which comprised 39 states and was established by the Congress of Vienna. The Confederation was designed to maintain the independence of individual states and therefore protect the status quo. While there was a central executive body, known as the Bundestag or Bund, it was dominated by Austria, whose emperor traditionally oversaw proceedings. Fundamentally, the Bund had very little power over the 39 states.

One area in which this was keenly felt was military weakness. The Federal Act, which had created the Bund, included the right for each of the 39 states to increase military cooperation. However, due to competing ideas, regional jealousies and powerful local particularism none of this was achieved. The defence of the Confederation depended on the continued cooperation of Austria and Prussia.

This caused a growth in nationalism, as many Germans were fearful of the growing military power of neighbouring countries, such as France and Russia, and especially resented the forced conscription of German soldiers into the French army. Increasingly, Germans believed that the only way to protect state security was through a united Germany and a combined army. This demonstrates that a fear of military weakness encouraged some Germans to turn to nationalism as a political solution.

On the other hand…

Although some Germans felt the impositions of the French were an inconvenience, the erosion of local particularism was too high a price to pay for a united Germany. Instead, some argued that Austria and Prussia were better able to protect the interests of the Bund and the 39 states. They argued that this was especially true after the defeat of Napoleon in 1815.

Overall

Clearly the foreign policy challenge posed by powerful neighbours was a material concern for many Germans. The French occupation of the German states had negatively impacted their development. The economic situation had grown worse with each year of occupation. The Continental Blockade, designed to economically isolate Britain through a trade embargo, caused severe constraints on consumption, and persistent warfare led to constant theft, looting and violence. Without a united nation-state and standing army, some argued that Germany's strategic concerns would never be realised, therefore contributing to the growth of nationalism.

1.1.4 Effects of the French Revolution and Napoleonic Wars

It was not only resentment toward French occupation that sparked a growth in nationalism but also the very ideals of the French Revolution itself. Moreover, there is an argument that the rationalisation of the German states under Napoleon's leadership laid the groundwork for a more modern and united Germany.

Ideas of the revolution

To some Germans, France was an inspirational example of what might be possible should Germany succeed in becoming a single nation-state. This was particularly true for German **liberals**. Unified France was viewed as a confident and powerful nation that dominated European politics. Additionally, many liberal Germans admired key French reforms. For example, the introduction of the Napoleonic Code ensured there was equality before the law and an end to autocratic and church privileges. This led to an increasing middle-class involvement in government and administration, as well as an end to feudal restrictions in France.

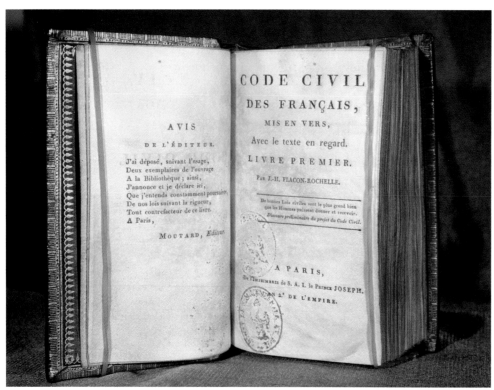

Figure 1.6 An original copy of the Napoleonic Code. This set out a collection of rules and laws that ushered in a more modern and equal system of government. Reforms like these were greatly admired by German liberals

This helps to explain why nationalism was attractive to many Germans, especially the growing middle class. The principles of the French Revolution removed ancient privilege and opened up access to the state to the professional middle-class French. This was hugely attractive to educated, middle-class Germans, who felt sidelined in the outdated feudal political structures of the old Holy Roman Empire. The ideals of the French Revolution inspired many of these Germans to agitate for a united Germany along the lines of post-revolution France.

Structural changes brought on by revolution

As well as introducing more modern ideas to the German states, French occupation encouraged states to progress from the structure of the Holy Roman Empire to the more rational 39 states of the German Confederation. In many ways, this laid the groundwork for the growth of German nationalism. As we have previously seen, the political system in Germany prior to the French Revolution revolved around the Holy Roman Empire, a loose federation of around 400 states of vastly different sizes and power. This disparate form emphasised and protected regional particularism, hindering the growth of nationalism. However, with French occupation came lasting change in the German states.

The French formally abolished the Holy Roman Empire in 1806 and formed the Confederation of the Rhine. This group consisted of 16 German states, including Bavaria, Baden, Hesse-Darmstadt and Württemberg. This not only led to the end of the Holy Roman Empire but reduced the number of German states overall to 39. Around 350 free imperial knights and counts lost their positions and were made subordinate to local rulers. A further 112 political units were abolished, including archbishops, abbeys and convents, and only six free cities remained.

This rapid political transition created a more modern system, which revealed the benefits of political cooperation. Moreover, the ending of ancient privilege and status opened the door to greater middle-class involvement in the state. Given that many middle-class Germans were predisposed to support unification and the ideals of the German Volk, nationalism began to flourish in the wake of the French Revolution.

On the other hand…

As the war against Napoleon's armies progressed to its conclusion in the early nineteenth century, German rulers appealed to nationalist sentiment in order to raise armies and drive out the French occupiers. Some historians argue, therefore, that any support for nationalism in the German states was temporary, a self-serving act on the part of the princes. For instance, once the French threat subsided, most German rulers returned to the traditional role of protecting their own self-interests.

Overall

While it may seem hyperbolic to echo T. Nipperdey's assertion that 'In the beginning there was Napoleon', it is clear that the French Revolution encouraged the growth of nationalism in Germany. French rule created the more modern framework in which nationalism could flourish and it showed the people the value of political cooperation, particularly the middle classes and liberal Germans who, inspired by the revolution, believed the German people could and should build their own nation-state.

M. Fulbrook sums up the change in Source 5.

> **SOURCE 5**
>
> Attacked, overrun, occupied, reorganised, exploited, provoked, shaken up, by 1815 Germany emerged in a very different shape; and the Holy Roman Empire, which had served as its loose political framework for so many centuries, had gone. The new settlement for Europe produced by the Congress of Vienna in 1814–15, which … was to inaugurate a very different period in Germany's history.
>
> **Fulbrook, M. (2019)** *A Concise History of Germany* **(3rd edn), Cambridge University Press**

1.1.5 Role of the liberals

Of considerable importance to growing nationalism was the development of liberalism, which took on an increasingly political form.

German liberals opposed the conservative rule of princes such as the Austrian chancellor Klemens von Metternich. Liberals sought to change the old-fashioned political and social structures of the German states and replace them with more modern, liberal ones. Many liberals believed this could be achieved through the creation of a united Germany. Given that Germany was undergoing significant social, economic and political change during this period, there is an argument that as the number of liberal-minded Germans grew, so too did German nationalism.

Growth and success of the liberals

German liberals sought the modernisation of Germany. They were drawn to ideas of parliamentary rule, individual freedoms and unification. These Germans were well-educated and wealthy members of the middle class, and they had seen their importance grow as the German states industrialised and developed. However, despite the fundamental importance of the middle classes, they remained excluded politically. This was in stark contrast to states like Britain and France. Many liberals saw the unification of Germany as a vehicle to deliver fundamental freedoms and rights. Moreover, it was often they who consumed the emerging nationalist ideas.

There were many liberal successes in the German states, arguably first sparked by the July Revolt in Paris in the 1830s, when the **reactionary** King Charles X of France was replaced with the more liberal Louis Philippe I. Further liberal successes included in Brunswick, where the ruling duke was driven out and his successor compelled to grant citizens a liberal **constitution**, and in Saxony and Hesse-Cassel, where liberal constitutions and laws were drawn up. In Baden, Bavaria and Württemberg liberal political parties gained parliamentary seats and successfully campaigned for greater press freedom. Similarly, Hanover granted a liberal constitution in 1832.

This caused a significant growth in nationalism, as liberals were able to apply pressure on the rulers of German states to bring about political change. The changes often enfranchised and protected the liberal middle class, who were now freer to call for a united Germany. Moreover, the representation of liberals in many state parliaments helped nationalism to spread, as they finally had a forum in which to agitate for a united Germany.

Liberalism in the 1840s

Nationalist sentiment grew during the crises of the 1840s. This was particularly evident when it looked like the French would again invade the German states along the Rhine river in an attempt to redraw the borders of the 1815 peace settlement. Although the French backed down, the events generated significant nationalist sentiment and liberals channelled this into calls for a united Germany. This was echoed in the German press, members of which overwhelmingly supported calls for a united nation in order to strengthen the states' ability to resist foreign powers. This period also generated a host of Romantic poetry and songs, such as 'Deutschland über alles', which were extremely popular with both liberal Germans and the wider public.

This pattern was repeated when Denmark threatened to **annex** the German-speaking areas of Schleswig and Holstein into the Danish kingdom. Schleswig was not part of the German Confederation, although it had a significant German-speaking minority. Holstein was predominantly German and a member of the Confederation. When the Danish king moved formally to incorporate these regions into Denmark, it sparked German outrage. Parliaments and rulers of nearly all German states criticised the plans so vociferously that the Danes decided to call off the planned annexation.

All of these events help to explain why nationalism grew in Germany between 1815 and 1850. Clearly, liberal ideas of a united Germany, a 'Fatherland' for Germans who shared a common language and history, were gaining in popularity. In addition, more states were adopting liberal constitutions and laws, further facilitating liberal calls for political modernisation. These sentiments were heightened during periods of external threat, such as from France and Denmark, when liberals and the press called for a united Germany so that Germans could resist the expansionist plans of more united neighbours.

On the other hand…

It would be wrong to view all liberals as united in their desires for a united Germany. For example, northern liberals were mostly conservative and defensive. They wanted to restore old estates while granting a small number of reforms to create a more modern legal structure. Southern liberals were generally more radical and sought new constitutions and limits to the power of rulers. This division made it harder for different groups of liberals to work together, limiting their impact on growing nationalism in Germany.

Moreover, some historians argue that once liberals had successfully introduced constitutions, laws and reforms within their own state, they no longer required a united Germany to secure their goals. Small in number, far from united, and separate from the majority of peasants and workers, it could therefore be argued that the liberals did not play a central role in the development of nationalism in Germany during this period.

Overall

Nonetheless, it is clear that liberals played at least some role in the growth of nationalism in Germany in the Vormärz period. Liberalism helped formalise and to an extent legitimise nationalist expression in the German states, and clearly liberals were successful in modernising the political frameworks of many states. That being said, it is likewise clear that the liberals were disunited, and still frequently loyal to local rulers, states and customs.

Why did German nationalism grow?

Clearly there were many factors that can help us understand the growth of nationalism in Germany.

The Romantic and philosophical ideas of nationalism played a role in encouraging the growth of nationalist thought, particularly among liberals and the German middle class. The idea of a German Volk gathered in a single state greatly appealed to many and caused a growing number of Germans, such as the members of student societies, clubs and national festivals, to celebrate 'Germanness' and call for a united Germany.

Some historians also point to the power and importance of economic cooperation, demonstrated through the successes of the Zollverein. Prussian economic dominance succeeded not only in increasing German economic power but also in excluding reactionary Austria. This tipped the balance of power between Austria and Prussia in favour of the latter, and allowed many Germans to witness the positive results of increased cooperation. If the German states could become more powerful through economic cooperation, could the same not be said for increased political unity?

Finally, it is clear that the effects of the French Revolution spurred nationalism in the German states, not only in those liberals who envied the political modernisation the revolution brought, but also among those who wanted a stronger, united Germany that would not fall prey to powerful neighbours.

ACTIVITIES

1 Write one sentence to define each of the following terms and groups:
   a) liberal
   b) reactionary
   c) aristocracy
   d) middle class

2 Select three pieces of evidence that demonstrate liberal successes.

3 There is an argument that the economic impact of the Zollverein was the most important reason why nationalism grew in Germany during this period, as it demonstrated how the German states could be more successful if they worked together.
   a) Select two to three pieces of evidence that support this argument.
   b) Explain how the evidence links to the argument, and supports the idea that the success of the Zollverein caused the growth in nationalism.
   c) Provide a counter-argument to this idea. Explain it in two to three sentences.
   d) Overall, argue how convincing this argument is as a reason for why nationalism grew in Germany during this period. Select an additional piece of evidence to back this up.

4 Create a timeline of events to signify growing nationalism in Germany, starting with 1789 and ending in 1850. Look for additional dates in this chapter and place them on the timeline. Then respond to these questions:
   a) Do you notice anything about the placement of the dates? Is there any pattern to them?
   b) Which decade may have been the most important in terms of growing nationalism? Why do you think this? What evidence is there?
   c) What were the critical moments in the growth of nationalism? Which events were most important? What caused those events?

5 Using the responses connected to your timeline, write an argument about what the main cause of the growth of nationalism was in Germany from 1815 to 1850.

GLOSSARY

Term	Meaning
annex	To add territory through appropriation.
aristocracy	The highest class in society, typically comprising people of noble birth holding hereditary titles and offices.
autonomy	The quality of being self-governing.
Burschenschaft (plural: Burschenschaften)	A student fraternity that advanced the cause of German nationalism.
constitution	A set of formal laws, often set out in one document, which govern how a state is run.
contiguous	Sharing a common, unbroken border.
Continental Blockade	A foreign policy blockade designed by Napoleon to weaken Britain during the Napoleonic Wars by placing embargoes on British trade.
crypto-nationalist	Someone who secretly supports nationalism, but keeps their beliefs hidden for fear of persecution.
customs duty	A charge set on goods sent abroad or to another German state. Also called a tariff.
Diet	An assembly or parliament. The German Imperial Diet was the deliberative body of the Holy Roman Empire.

Term	Meaning
executive	The branch of government responsible for putting decisions or laws into effect.
Habsburg	The dynasty that ruled Austria between 1278 and 1918.
industrialisation	The development of industries in a country or region on a wide scale.
liberal	Relating to or denoting a political and social philosophy that promotes individual rights, civil liberties, democracy and free enterprise.
nation-state	A sovereign state in which most of the citizens or subjects are united by factors that define a nation, such as language or common descent.
particularism	Exclusive attachment to one's own state, traditions or the history of a particular region.
primordial	Existing since the beginning of time.
reactionary	Someone who opposes political or social progress or reform.
republican	A person who believes in a state in which citizens, rather than a monarch or a small ruling class, hold the power. A republican state is one in which the people and their elected representatives hold the power.
Romantic movement	An artistic, literary, musical and intellectual movement that originated in Europe during the late eighteenth and early nineteenth centuries. It celebrated nature and the past over civilisation and industrialisation, and valued imagination and emotion over rationality.
serfdom	A system through which agricultural labourers are bound to the aristocratic estates in which they work.
sovereignty	Supreme power or authority.
standing army	A permanent army of paid soldiers.
status quo	The existing state of affairs.
Volk	The German people.
Vormärz	The period of German history between 1815 and 1848 characterised by the dominance of Austria and Prussia.

Chapter 2

An assessment of the degree of growth of nationalism in Germany, up to 1850

The aim of this chapter is to evaluate the extent to which nationalism had grown in Germany by 1850.

LINK TO EXAM

Higher

Key issue 2: This chapter will weigh up how much nationalism had actually grown in particular areas, allowing pupils to judge by how much nationalism had actually grown by 1850.

Background

It is clear from the discussion in Chapter 1 that there were many factors which caused the growth of nationalism in Germany. Economically, the growing strength of Prussia, the success of the **Zollverein** and the increasingly interconnected transport and communications infrastructure inspired calls for a united Germany. Cultural factors were similarly significant, and a common language, history and heritage encouraged many writers, thinkers and poets to call for a united home for the German **Volk**. **Liberals** were likewise frequent in their calls for unification, in hopes that it would enable them to advance their cause – the formation of a modern, **constitutional** Germany. The effects of the French Revolution and German military weakness also encouraged some Germans to push for a united Germany as the only way to guarantee state security.

However, while these factors all bolstered a growing German nationalism, there has been much debate as to how much it had actually grown by 1850. Was Germany on the verge of forming a united **nation-state**? Or was this simply a fascination of a small number of highly educated Germans, removed from the day-to-day concerns of workers and peasants?

This chapter will assess how much nationalism, that is the desire to form a united Germany, had grown. First, we will discuss the supporters of nationalism: the educated middle class and liberals. Second, we will outline the role played by the opponents of nationalism, for example those engaging in local particularism as well as the **conservative** and **reactionary** Austria. Finally, we will set out the events of the 1840s, including turmoil, revolution and the collapse of the emergent Frankfurt Parliament.

Traditional historical research has classified this period in Germany as one of nationalist growth, albeit limited, as the historian H. W. Smith points out (Source 1).

SOURCE 1

Historical research has traditionally considered the years from 1800 onwards to mark the era of the development of German nationalism. Yet, until 1848, nationalism in Germany evolved into a political movement only partially ... It was not until the founding of Imperial Germany in 1871 that continuous political movements started to develop.

Smith, H. W. (2015) *The Oxford Handbook of Modern German History*, **Oxford University Press**

However, while there is an argument that German nationalism would not enjoy broad support until 1871 onwards (see Chapter 4), clearly the Germany of 1850 was a different place to the Germany of 1815. The evidence in this chapter will help you to analyse and assess the degree to which nationalism had grown in Germany by 1850.

2.1 How much had nationalism grown in Germany by 1850?

For the purposes of the examination, it is important to be able to analyse how much nationalism had grown in Germany by 1850. This chapter will help you to do this through the assessment of various groups and events, enabling you to make a judgement on this question.

It is important to note that there is a great deal of overlap between the information in this chapter and in Chapters 1 and 3. This is deliberate, and will help support you in responding to questions. The information in the first three chapters covers the same period of history, so it is important to ensure that you are responding to the correct question, be it the causes of the growth of nationalism (Chapter 1), the extent to which nationalism had grown by 1850 (Chapter 2), or the barriers to the growth of nationalism (Chapter 3). You should read all three chapters to get the most out of the information provided.

This section will examine the following factors:

Supporters of nationalism
Opponents of nationalism
Political turmoil in the 1840s
Frankfurt Parliament
Collapse of revolution in Germany, 1848–49

Understanding these issues will allow you to make a judgement on how much German nationalism had grown by 1850.

2.1.1 Supporters of nationalism

There was a high degree of support for nationalism among the educated middle class and liberals. Members of the middle class were often consumers of Romantic ideas and believed in the creation of a German nation-state that would become the spiritual homeland for the Volk, those Germans who some believed were a **primordial** people with a shared language, history and culture. Liberals were more influenced by the economic success of institutions such as the Zollverein. They argued that a united Germany could bring even greater prosperity if this success were to be emulated politically. Though small in number, both groups made popular and effective calls for unification.

It is important to note that the educated middle class and liberals were not mutually exclusive categories. All liberals were from the educated middle class, but not all middle-class Germans were liberals. Liberal Germans were those who wanted to expand political and civil rights as well as progress economic deregulation.

Educated middle class

Perhaps the most fervent advocates of a united Germany were the educated middle classes. These Germans consumed the ideas of the Romantic movement that were part of the German literary revival. Well-known writers, poets and thinkers such as Johann Fichte, Georg Hegel and Johann Herder supported this view and argued that the Germans were unique. Ernst Arndt wrote accessible pamphlets calling for the creation of a German 'Vaterland', or 'Fatherland'. Other writers, like the Brothers Grimm, collected and published folk stories and oral histories that were presented as being naturally 'German', rather than belonging to the people of a particular state. This was seen to prove the idea that the Germans were a primordial people who were unique in their efforts to preserve their linguistic and cultural history, which helped to give the German elite a sense of cultural leadership.

This shows that there had been a significant growth of nationalism among the educated middle class. This type of cultural nationalism gave way to a kind of ethnic nationalism, through which the German Volk were regarded more highly than people of other communities. This 'special' nature of the German people led many in the educated middle class to call for all Germans to live in a united nation-state – in other words, the cultural nation, the Volk, should have a political nation, a united Germany. This suggests there were pervasive nationalist ideas among members of the middle class.

There is additional evidence to suggest that there had been a significant growth of nationalism among the educated middle class. One such example relates to student movements and national festivals. The historian C. Jansen outlines the nature of some of these groups (Source 2).

SOURCE 2

After the end of the Holy Roman Empire and the defeat of Napoleon, organized nationalism gradually emerged, and turned into a social movement: during the 1810s, between 1830 and 1832, and during the years of the Revolution 1848–49 … As a social movement, German nationalism was based on two types of interrelated organization: manifestly and latently political … [and] Publicly operating clubs and societies, with the national festival one of the most significant expressions of organized nationalism.

Jansen, C. (2015) 'The Formation of German Nationalism, 1740–1850', in H. W. Smith (ed.) *The Oxford Handbook of Modern German History*, **Oxford University Press**

At the beginning of the nineteenth century, nationalism increasingly appealed to the educated middle class. Calls for a united Germany were expressed in club meetings and at national festivals. Student fraternities, or **Burschenschaften**, were created to inspire patriotism. These were complemented by the crypto-nationalist gymnastic groups set up by Friedrich Ludwig Jahn. The first Burschenschaft was founded in Jena in June 1815, and after three years had over 4000 members. A confederation of 14 German universities joined the General Association of German Fraternities in the same year. By 1818, there were almost 18,000 full and part-time members. The nationalist desires for a united Germany were likewise on display during the Wartburg Festival in 1817, where 500 nationalist students turned the gathering into a demonstration against the German princes and **absolute rule**.

These groups featured large membership and influential participants. It therefore appears reasonable to argue that nationalism and the ideals of a united Germany had spread to a significant extent within the educated middle class.

Figure 2.1 The Wartburg Festival in 1817. Festivals such as this one became popular occasions for nationalist demonstrations. Although the number of participants was arguably relatively small, the festivals were deemed to be a serious threat by members of the ruling elite, such as the Austrian chancellor Metternich

Finally, we must acknowledge the success of the Zollverein when examining the extent of nationalist growth among the educated middle class. When the Zollverein was formed in 1834 it encouraged economic cooperation between erstwhile relatively disparate German states. It was formed when Bavaria and Württemberg joined the Prussian **Customs Union**. This union removed trade barriers and abolished internal **tariffs**. By 1844, the Zollverein included all major German states. It encouraged significant economic growth, and soon Prussia was the dominant economy among the German states. Importantly, this success was achieved without the involvement of Austria, which had traditionally dominated German politics and acted to limit the growth of German power.

The growth of economic cooperation between German states was seen by those educated middle class involved in business and industry as particularly meaningful. The success of the Zollverein proved what could be achieved if the states could cooperate and limit the influence of Austria. Therefore, many middle-class Germans supported political nationalism as a way of advancing their economic interests.

Liberals

Likewise, there is evidence to suggest a significant growth of nationalism among liberal Germans. This group desired, above all else, an end to the absolute rule of the German princes. Inspired by the modern ideas of the French Revolution and the impact of reforms such as the Napoleonic Code, they called for parliamentary rule, individual freedoms and a united Germany. They desired the establishment of a strong, liberal German nation-state that would instil these freedoms across all German states. Most liberals did not approve of a universal franchise. Rather, they hoped to reform the state to give more access to the highly educated, skilled and growing middle class.

While the primary aim of liberally minded Germans was the creation of a liberal Germany, this meant by default that many wanted to advance a united Germany as a vehicle for delivering this goal. As A. Farmer states, 'virtually all German liberals were nationalists'. This supports the argument that nationalism among liberal Germans had grown to a significant extent.

On the other hand…

There are limitations to the argument that there had been a significant growth of nationalism based on the actions of middle-class Germans alone. First, it is important to note that the educated middle class, though vocal in their calls for a united Germany, were a small minority within the social structure of the German states at the time. The majority of Germans were agricultural workers, who arguably had little interest in the intellectual discourse of the period. G. Mann sums this up when he argues that most Germans 'did not look up from the plough'.

Additionally, while social movements such as student clubs and national festivals provided a means for advancing nationalist ideas, Metternich quickly shut them down. Deeply concerned about what he viewed as dangerous German nationalism in the wake of the murder of German dramatist August von Kotzebue by militant nationalist student Karl Ludwig Sand, Metternich and a conference of state princes enacted the Carlsbad Decrees in 1819. The decrees, **ratified** in the German **Bundestag**, dissolved the Burschenschaften and clamped down on the liberal press. This suggests that the degree of nationalist growth may have been limited. Not only were the decrees supported by the German states, but they also limited the ability of these groups to operate and sustain their calls for a united Germany.

Figure 2.2 Klemens von Metternich was Austrian chancellor from 1821 to 1848. As the former foreign minister, he had played a huge role in the Vienna peace settlement. During the revolutions of 1848–49 he was forced to flee Austria, and settled in London

Finally, although liberal Germans were almost exclusively nationalist, the movement was divided. During this period, constitutions were drawn up in Bavaria and Baden in 1818, Württemberg in 1819, and Hesse-Darmstadt in 1820. Once these liberals had succeeded in bringing an end to absolute rule in their own states, they felt less of a need to call for a united Germany since they had achieved their aims locally. Moreover, there remained divisions between the more conservative liberals in the north and the more **radical** liberals in the south. This is perhaps evidence that the growth of nationalism among liberal Germans was far from extensive, as some were satisfied with the progress made in their own states.

Overall

Nevertheless, it is fair to say that, although they were small in number, there had been a significant growth of nationalist thought among the educated middle class and liberals. The Romantic movement and student bodies encouraged unification, while liberal Germans sought a strong Germany which would deliver individual freedoms to the emerging industrial middle class. Indeed, even though Metternich took swift action against these groups, calls for a united Germany did not cease. During the 1830s there was a profusion of folk festivals, which emphasised the importance of German culture and the idea of a German Volk. In 1832, around 30,000 Germans gathered at the Hambach Festival to hear nationalist speeches, wave yellow, black and gold flags, and drink toasts to the idea of a united Germany, all of which gives credence to the argument that there was a significant degree of nationalist growth among the educated middle class and liberals.

23

2.1.2 Opponents of nationalism

While there were clearly many in the German states who felt passionately that Germany should unite, there were many who were equally passionate in their opposition to growing nationalism. They included those who fought for the continuing particularism of the German states, with the aim to retain the different cultural traditions and powers across the states. They also included Austria, staunchly conservative and opposed to any growth in German power, particularly if it challenged Austria's political dominance over the 39 states.

The particularism of the German states

We could argue that the continuing particularism of the German states suggests there had not been a significant growth of nationalism in Germany by 1850.

Prior to the French Revolution, the German states had been under the rule of the Holy Roman Empire. This was a confederation of nearly 400 states of varying size and importance. When these states were defeated by the French in the wake of the French Revolution, Napoleon reformed this system. The Confederation of the Rhine dissolved the medieval Holy Roman Empire and created a confederation of 16 German states. It was these states that formed the basis of the German Confederation in 1815 after the defeat of Napoleon.

However, as the historian A. Farmer points out (Source 3), the creation of the German Confederation was not designed to promote the case for a united Germany but rather to maintain the status quo.

> ### SOURCE 3
>
> The Confederation was not concerned with promoting a united Germany. In fact, its aim was exactly the opposite, for none of the rulers of the separate states wished to see his independence limited by the establishment of a strong, central German government.
>
> **Farmer, A. (2020)** *Access to History: The Unification of Germany and the Challenge of Nationalism 1789–1919*, **Hodder Education**

There were significant differences between the German states. For example, the majority of the northern states were Protestant, while those in the south were Catholic. Northern and eastern Germany were mostly autocratic and conservative, while the west and south were more liberal and progressive. Local dialects and customs persisted, while the northern economies were predominantly agricultural versus the industrialising west. With no strong central government being established in 1815, this created a situation where state rulers could retain their power and position.

This suggests that the degree to which nationalism had grown in Germany by 1850 was in fact limited. The political system created in 1815 lent itself to the particularism of individual states. This meant that local rulers and princes could retain all of their powers and rights without fear of losing them to a united Germany. Given that these princes were overwhelmingly in favour of retaining their power, this suggests that the growth of nationalism was limited, particularly due to the political system created in 1815.

Austria

While regional particularism suggests there had been only a limited growth of nationalism in Germany up to 1850, Austria also had a part to play in slowing its spread.

Austria was a powerful force in European politics and had played a significant role in the defeat of Napoleon and the ensuing peace settlement in 1815. Indeed, Klemens von Metternich perhaps played the most significant part in the formation of the German Confederation, due to his concern that if Germany was to unite and form a nation-state it would immediately challenge Austria's position in Europe. Therefore, in his role as Austria's chief minister at the Vienna peace settlement, he helped design a German political system that was intended to maintain the status quo. The German states accepted this arrangement and were willing to allow conservative Austria to continue to dominate German politics. For example, the German Confederation had only one **executive** body, the Bundestag, which met in Frankfurt am Main. While each of the 39 German states sent a representative, the body was presided over by the Austrian representative, in recognition of the traditional power held by the **Habsburg** emperors. The Bundestag became little more than a conservative organ to promote and protect the interests of individual states and the primacy of Austrian political power over the German states.

This perhaps suggests there had not been a significant degree of nationalist growth in Germany, as it is clear that state rulers were content to go along with the status quo if it meant retaining their own powers and traditional status, despite the continued political dominance of Austria. Given that the princes were often absolute rulers and members of established, aristocratic families, it is clear that the ideas of nationalism had not penetrated the upper classes of society. Therefore, it seems fair to argue that despite the growth of nationalism among liberals and the middle class, the same could not be said for those in the German states who operated the levers of power. This suggests that perhaps nationalism had only grown to a small extent in Germany by 1850.

On the other hand…

On the other hand, we could argue that the strength of regional particularism was waning by 1850. This was primarily driven by the growth of interconnected transport networks, spurred on by the success of economic integration. Roads, canals and, crucially, rail networks connected German states that had been hitherto isolated and insular. This allowed for the spread of increasingly popular literature, pamphlets and ideas. This limits the argument that particularism hampered the growth of nationalism in Germany.

Moreover, Austria's power was waning, as it faced its own challenges from different national groups within its multinational borders, as evidenced by the revolutions of 1848 in cities such as Vienna and Budapest.

Overall

Nevertheless, we could argue that the powerful opponents to nationalism reveal it was not widespread by 1850. Clearly those with power during this period, including local rulers and the Austrian emperors, had a vested interest in maintaining the status quo. That the state representatives of the Bundestag were willing to support Austria's introduction of the suppressive Carlsbad Decrees in 1819 demonstrates they were more interested in preserving their own power than indulging in any concept of a German nation-state. Moreover, the German conservative slogan 'Authority not majority' highlights the rulers' desire to reject ideas of nationalism in favour of the traditional, established authority set out in the German Confederation.

2.1.3 Political turmoil in the 1840s

The 1840s were a period of tremendous stress and tension across Europe, and especially in Germany. These issues manifested in extreme social and economic problems (especially for workers and peasants), foreign policy challenges from Denmark and France, and an increase in the number of challenges to traditional authority. Some historians use these events as evidence to argue that a growing number of Germans were dissatisfied with their lives and had grown attracted to the idea of nationalism as a vehicle for improving conditions.

Worker and peasant discontent

The historian M. Fulbrook outlines the problems that many Germans faced in the crises of the 1840s (Source 4).

> **SOURCE 4**
>
> Further socioeconomic changes were occurring which were to feed into immediate political upheavals. In Europe as a whole, population expansion had been taking place since the mid-eighteenth century. European population approximately doubled between the mid-eighteenth century and the mid-nineteenth century. In Germany, much of the population growth was rural; and the food supply of a still pre-industrial economy proved insufficient to support a growing population on the land. Food riots, rural unemployment, migration to the growing towns, even emigration to America were common.
>
> **Fulbrook, M. (2019)** *A Concise History of Germany* (3rd edn), **Cambridge University Press**

The number of cases of workers acting to improve their own conditions was on the increase. For example, in 1844, Silesian weavers staged a revolt to protest against cheaper British imports damaging their industry. This was compounded by a **potato blight** in 1846–47, which led to malnutrition and starvation for many and thousands of deaths from poverty-related diseases. It also led to a sharp increase in food prices and a reduction in consumer spending that further damaged the rural and urban economies alike. This burgeoning social unrest coincided with growing liberal and middle-class concerns that conservatives in Austria and among the German aristocracy were holding Germany back.

This suggests there had been a significant growth of nationalism. The events of the 1840s saw an increasing scepticism among workers and peasants towards the system established in the German Confederation being able to support a modern and growing socioeconomic system. Many rulers were seen to be incompetent and ill-equipped for modern-world challenges. Therefore, some German workers and peasants turned to nationalism as a strategy for removing incompetent princes and creating a modern, united Germany that could better meet their economic and social needs.

External threats

Foreign policy crises in the 1840s sparked a strong nationalist response, which suggests that there was in fact a growing level of nationalism in Germany up to 1850.

The first crisis emerged in 1840, when it appeared that France would invade the German states in order to redraw the border around the Rhine area. As French calls for military action grew stronger, so too did the German nationalist reaction. Many Germans were horrified at the thought of renewed French military action, which harked back to French control of the German states and the formation of the Confederation of the Rhine in 1806. The response sparked outrage, for example through nationalist poetry and songs such as 'Deutschland über alles'. The press supported and encouraged this nationalist surge, printing nationalist stories, songs and poems that were rapturously received by the German public.

In 1848, the King of Denmark prompted further outrage when he announced his plans to formally integrate Schleswig and Holstein into the Kingdom of Denmark. Holstein in particular was predominantly German-speaking, and was a formal member of the German Confederation. The German response was so profound that the Danes retracted their plans to annex these lands and stood down.

This suggests that there was in fact a significant degree of nationalist growth in Germany. The fact that, when threatened, Germans from different states appeared to unite in response to external aggression suggests there was an increasingly popular idea of Germany as a united country. This was apparently particularly important given that a divided Germany appeared weak and unable to resist the machinations of neighbouring states. That the reaction to these foreign policy events was so pronounced suggests that nationalism had indeed grown to a significant extent by 1850.

On the other hand…

When considering the economic and social crises of the 1840s, some historians argue that although there may have been a slight increase in nationalist ideas among workers and peasants, this was only temporary. This argument centres on the idea that workers and peasants, faced with terrible conditions and hardships, wanted only to improve their immediate conditions. Once the turmoil of the 1840s was over and socioeconomic conditions had improved, the level of nationalist support among these groups waned. This suggests that the events of the 1840s were not, in fact, a sign of significant or lasting increase in nationalism among the workers and peasants.

Similarly, the nationalism prompted by foreign policy challenges during the 1840s appears to have decreased once the crises were over, suggesting there was perhaps only a limited growth of nationalism in general by 1850.

Overall

What is clear is that Germany was changing socially and economically. It was urbanising quickly. For example, Berlin's population had risen to 172,000 in 1800 and by 1848 it had increased to 410,000. The problems connected with rapid industrialisation, urbanisation and the crises of the 1840s certainly led to an increasing number of Germans questioning the rule of incompetent princes. Moreover, a growth in nationalist sentiment was particularly visible during times of foreign threat. When viewed together, these factors do suggest there had been a significant growth of nationalism by 1850, although there is some debate as to whether this growth was a short-term reaction to an external threat or a sustained growth resulting from a fundamentally changed way of thinking.

2.1.4 Frankfurt Parliament

1848 is a key year when assessing the degree to which nationalism had grown in Germany by 1850. Although tensions in the German states had been rising during the turmoil of the 1840s, the urban poor, peasants and liberals were disunited and did not have collective aims or objectives. However, in February 1848, King Louis Philippe of France was overthrown and a republic was established in France. This event impacted the whole of Europe, including Germany. The reverberations were quickly felt in Mannheim in Baden, where liberals demanded a liberal constitution and individual freedoms. Under pressure, the Grand Duke of Baden refused the aid of Prussian troops and reformed his government to include liberal ministers.

Austria was likewise shaken by revolution and Metternich was forced to flee under pressure from mass demonstrations. The country faced extreme challenges in nearly every region across the empire, **feudal** landlords were attacked and there was a general breakdown of law and order. As the news reached Berlin, and under pressure following popular unrest, Prussian king Frederick William IV marched through the streets in the national colours of red, gold and black. By March 1848 many German rulers were anxious that their power and authority would be challenged, and so gave way to liberal demands. It was in this power vacuum that the Frankfurt Parliament was set up.

Figure 2.3 An image of the burning of the throne of King Louis Philippe during the French revolution of 1848. This event sparked a series of revolutions across Germany and Europe

Achievements of the Parliament

In March 1848, delegations from Baden, Bavaria, Frankfurt, Nassau, Prussia and Württemberg met in Heidelberg and agreed to the formation of a Vorparlament, or 'preparatory' parliament, with the aim to arrange for the election of an all-German parliament. The Vorparlament quickly agreed to elect a national parliament that would draw up a national constitution of Germany. These elections were carried out peacefully, with around 85 per cent of men eligible to vote.

The parliament first met in May 1848 and consisted of 585 members, the vast majority of whom were middle class. In fact, it was dubbed the 'Professors' Parliament', as over 80 per cent of its representatives held a university degree. Despite divisions, the parliament was able to agree on several key issues which suggested that nationalist sentiment, and the willingness of states to contribute nationally, had grown by a significant degree.

One of the Frankfurt Parliament's greatest achievements was majority agreement over the so-called Fifty Articles. The articles included a commitment to equality before the law, individual freedoms and an end to class discrimination.

By March 1849, after a great deal of discussion and debate, the parliament finally agreed to a German Constitution by 267 votes to 263. This constitution called for two houses, the lower democratically elected and the upper made up of existing German princes and monarchs. These houses would control legislation and finance. There would be a German emperor with considerable power, although they would hold this office for a specific period of time.

All of these achievements and agreements suggest that nationalism in Germany had grown to a significant extent by 1850. The fact that a majority of Germans agreed not only to form a parliament but on the specifics of individual rights and the constitution shows a tremendous degree of cooperation and collaboration, despite the notable challenges of the period. Germans, it appeared, were willing to set aside regional particularism and discuss the creation of a single German political unit. Taken together, this suggests that there was a significant growth of nationalism in Germany by 1850.

On the other hand…

Despite the noteworthy achievements of the Frankfurt Parliament, it was hindered by division and disagreement. The parliament was particularly criticised by Marxists, such as Friedrich Engels. One criticism was that the discussions in parliament were unnecessarily abstract. Indeed, the first six months of discussions revolved around which rights individuals should be granted. This delayed the more pressing issue of the creation of a legal German Constitution.

Moreover, parliament's success was only made possible as the conservative states of Prussia and Austria were preoccupied with managing revolution. Had they been less preoccupied, it is highly likely that these reactionary states would have acted to suppress radical nationalism.

Additionally, without money, tax-raising powers, an army or a strong executive power, the Frankfurt Parliament was fundamentally limited in its ability to deliver the reforms the peasants and workers strongly desired. This limited its legitimacy and made it appear to be a vehicle for delivering only what liberal and middle-class Germans wanted.

Given the limitations and challenges the parliament faced, some historians argue that in fact nationalism had only grown to a certain extent by 1850. Had there been a greater desire to forge a united Germany, discussions would likely have been faster and more decisive. The nature of the parliament and its decisions suggest that maybe German nationalism was not widespread among the educated middle class.

Overall

It appears that the German states only accepted the formation of the Frankfurt Parliament because they feared their thrones were in danger, given the revolutionary atmosphere of 1848–49. Many rulers feared that by opposing the parliament they would stir up opposition to their own regimes. They were therefore willing to allow the parliament to operate in the short term, not because of growing nationalist sentiment but due to political expediency. The achievements of the Frankfurt Parliament were only possible as a result of having this political space in which to operate.

However, as conservative forces regained their authority in Austria, Prussia and the German states more generally, the power of the parliament waned and, ultimately, by 1849 all of the hopes of the parliament had ended. This suggests that perhaps there had not been a significant growth of nationalism in Germany, rather that middle-class and liberal Germans had been able to advance the cause of nationalism during a period when political opposition to nationalism had been removed.

2.1.5 Collapse of revolution in Germany, 1848–49

While many nationalist thinkers might have hoped the short-term successes of 1848–49 reflected a high degree of nationalist growth, this is arguably not the case. For example, as conservative forces in and around Germany regained their strength, it became clear that few were willing or powerful enough to be able to stand up for the idea of a united Germany. Given that the revolution of 1848 collapsed, and conservative forces regained their former power, some historians argue that nationalism in Germany had only grown to a slight extent.

Failure of Prussia to support nationalism

As we have already seen, Prussia was the dominant power among the German states. However, Prussia did not act to support German nationalism, instead choosing to introduce local reforms and suppress the growth of nationalism across the states more generally. This suggests that, given the largest German state was seemingly not in favour of a united, liberal Germany, perhaps the extent of nationalist growth in general was limited.

King Frederick William IV had long been a friend and ally to Austria's chancellor Metternich. Both rulers had prioritised the maintenance of the status quo and opposed the forces of revolution and reform. However, in 1848 and under significant pressure, King Friedrich chose to appoint a liberal ministry and agreed to the election of an assembly to draw up a new constitution. The Prussian Parliament was disunited, although it did manage to achieve important reforms in rural regions, such as ending the feudal privileges of the Junker class.

Figure 2.4 The Prussian Junkers were the landed nobility of Prussia. They owned huge rural estates that were worked by large numbers of peasants. They were primarily interested in maintaining their own power and hereditary rights

However, these moves prompted a strong conservative reaction in Prussia. Prussian landowners formed local associations to resist the threat of reform posed by the new Prussian Parliament. For example, in 1848 the League for the Protection of Landed Property met in Berlin and was called the Junker Parliament. It argued that any reforms should come from the king, not the 'masses'.

By the summer of 1848, it appeared that many Prussians were losing their appetite for a united Germany. The king regained control of foreign policy and made peace with Denmark, much to the anger of the Frankfurt Parliament. By August, Austria was regaining control of its empire and, encouraged by this, King Friedrich shut down the Prussian Parliament and fired liberal ministers. By November 1848 the new minister of the interior, Count Brandenburg, had declared martial law and closed down political clubs and meetings. There was almost no resistance to these counter-revolutionary moves, and on 5 December 1848 Frederick proclaimed his own constitution for Prussia.

Therefore, Prussia, the dominant German state, did not seem to reflect the nationalist ideas emerging in other parts of Germany. The fact that the general population of Prussia had neither the power nor the will to press for a united Germany during the collapse of the 1848 revolution seems to support the argument that there had not been a significant growth of nationalism by 1850.

Lack of support from the peasantry

Moreover, it appeared as if there was a general lack of support for nationalism in the collapse of the 1848 revolution, which also suggests there had not been a significant growth of nationalism in Germany up to 1850.

One example of this was the narrow base of support for a united Germany, which was largely confined to the educated middle class and liberals and did not appear to be mirrored in other parts of German society. The historian M. S. Anderson highlights this point (Source 5).

SOURCE 5

The revolutions suffered from the narrowness of their social base. In particular the dislike felt by the peasant for educated urban revolutionaries who pursued objectives which he did not understand and was not expected to understand showed itself almost everywhere. For a moment one of the greatest of the submerged social resentments of the eighteenth and first half of the nineteenth centuries, that of the countryside for the increasingly dominant and apparently exploiting town, showed itself with unusual clarity.

Anderson, M. S. (1972) *The Ascendancy of Europe 1815–1914*, **Longman**

This suggests there was no broad support for the ideas of a united Germany expressed by educated, urban Germans. For example, the desires and demands of the peasants were different to those of the middle classes, and they did not align with nationalism. Indeed, the harvests of 1847 and 1848 were considered of reasonably good quality, helping to meet the immediate demands of rural peasants. Moreover, as many of the German states, including Prussia, abolished many feudal traditions and privileges during the 1848 revolutions, the majority of peasants appeared unwilling to support nationalist ideas, as their political demands had been mostly met. Indeed, nationalist ideas seemed to be in the interest of urban revolutionaries and middle-class liberals, rather than the rural peasant.

The majority of the population appeared to have little interest in supporting the nationalist agenda. With sufficient harvests and the abolition of some outdated feudal powers, the appetite among the peasants for a nationalist revolution waned. Moreover, the failure of the peasants to support the revolution of 1848 was crucial. Taken together, this appears to suggest that there had not been a significant growth of nationalism in Germany by 1850.

The recovery of Austria and the conservatives

The recovery of Austria and the German conservatives in 1848–49 also suggests that the ideas of German nationalism had not grown significantly by 1850. In October 1848, Austrian forces had effectively regrouped and regained control of their empire. Two thousand people were killed in Vienna as government forces regained control. By 1849 the Habsburgs had dissolved their parliament in Austria, regained total control of their empire and imposed martial law in areas where there had been vocal calls for liberalism. It was clear that the forces of reaction were rising, and the political situation reverted to one in which politics in central and eastern Europe was once again dominated by conservative Prussia, Austria and Russia.

Again, this suggests that there had been no significant rise in nationalism. The forces hoping for a united Germany were, it seems, disunited, did not enjoy popular support, and were supressed and undermined by powerful states which had no interest in allowing for the spread of nationalist ideas. Taken as a whole, this appears to suggest there had been no significant growth of nationalism in Germany by 1850.

On the other hand...

The revolutions of 1848 did bring change to the German states, and perhaps Prussia in particular. When King Frederick William IV announced the new Prussian constitution on 5 December 1848, he cleverly reflected many of the liberal demands in this new set of laws. While the constitution was neither wholly liberal nor nationalist, it did address many of the demands of the liberals and nationalists, including several important individual freedoms, a Prussian Parliament and a limitation to the power of the king. This suggests that pressures from liberals and nationalists had brought about a degree of change in Germany by 1850.

Overall

Within a few months of the 1848 revolution, it was clear that national support for a united Germany was diminishing. The slow progress of the Frankfurt Parliament and the divisions among those calling for a united Germany were apparently too hard to overcome. It seems fair to argue that no national consciousness had emerged. Members of the German states remained loyal to their local region, rather than committed to the notion of a united Germany. Additionally, Prussian troops were active in supressing nationalist expression in other German states. For example, in 1849 there were uprisings in Saxony and the Rhenish Palatinate in support of liberal constitutions. Prussian troops were deployed to crush these uprisings. This suggests local particularism and a desire to protect the regional status quo remained strong.

However, it would be incorrect to assert that nothing had changed, as the historian M. Fulbrook highlights (Source 6).

SOURCE 6

It is a curious revolution to evaluate. National unification was manifestly not achieved: it foundered on the rocks of regional particularism, the unwillingness of sovereigns to subsume their sovereignty in a wider entity, and the facts of power politics. Liberals possessed both too little real power, and too little popular support, to be able to put through their programme: they were on many issues divided amongst themselves. But it was not a revolution without consequences. Feudal social relations on the land, effectively abolished all over Germany by 1850, did not return. The particular system of political repression associated with Metternich did not return ... and there was the formation of a range of national groupings and political orientations.

Fulbrook, M. (2019) *A Concise History of Germany* (3rd edn), Cambridge University Press

How much had nationalism grown in Germany by 1850?

Therefore, it is clear that there is some evidence to suggest that nationalism had grown significantly in Germany by 1850. Among liberal and middle-class Germans, often inspired by the ideals of the Romantic movement or the empirical evidence of the benefits of cooperation, there was a significant growth in nationalist sentiment. However, the same could not be said of the peasantry and aristocracy who, for different reasons, either did not support or did not actively oppose the ideas of nationalism. The failures of the Frankfurt Parliament and the 1848 revolution appear to support the idea that, up to 1850, nationalism had not grown significantly in Germany.

ACTIVITIES

1 Select three pieces of evidence which support the argument that there had been a significant growth of nationalism in Germany by 1850.

2 Select three pieces of evidence which support the argument that there had not been a significant growth of nationalism in Germany by 1850.

3 Create a visual sketch of a set of scales.
   a) Include all evidence that suggests there had been a significant growth of nationalism on one side of the scales.
   b) Include all evidence that suggests there had not been a significant growth of nationalism on the other side of the scales.

4 Judge the degree to which you find it convincing that nationalism had grown in Germany by 1850. Include three or more reasons why you think this.

5 Copy and complete the following table.

Factor	Evidence to support the fact that there was a significant growth of nationalism	Evidence to support the fact that there was not a significant growth of nationalism	Overall, how much had nationalism grown in this area?
Supporters			
Opponents			
Turmoil of the 1840s			
Frankfurt Parliament			
Collapse of revolution, 1848			

Term	Meaning
absolute rule	A form of power in which the ruler, often a king, holds supreme autocratic authority.
Bundestag	The parliament of the German Confederation, which came into existence as a result of the Congress of Vienna in 1815.
Burschenschaft (plural: Burschenschaften)	A student fraternity that advanced the cause of German nationalism.
conservative	Someone averse to change or who holds traditional values.
constitution	A set of formal laws, often set out in one document, which govern how a state is run.
customs union	A group of states that reduce or eliminate taxes to allow the free movement of goods.
executive	The branch of government responsible for putting decisions or laws into effect.
feudal	A system in which the nobility owns the land on which agricultural workers work.
Habsburg	The dynasty that ruled Austria between 1278 and 1918.
liberal	Relating to or denoting a political and social philosophy that promotes individual rights, civil liberties, democracy and free enterprise.
nation-state	A sovereign state in which most of the citizens or subjects are united by factors that define a nation, such as language or common descent.
potato blight	A destructive fungal disease that rots potatoes.
primordial	Existing since the beginning of time.
radical	Someone who supports complete political or social change.
ratification	The action of signing or giving formal consent to a treaty, contract or agreement, making it officially valid.
reactionary	Someone who opposes political or social progress or reform.
tariff	A tax or duty to be paid on a particular class of imported or exported goods.
Volk	The German people.
Zollverein	A customs union of German states formed to manage tariffs and economic policies. It was created by the 1833 Zollverein treaties and formally started on 1 January 1834.

Chapter 3

An evaluation of the obstacles to German unification, 1815–50

The aim of this chapter is to evaluate the obstacles to the unification of Germany between 1815 and 1850.

LINK TO EXAM

Higher

Key issue 3: this chapter will examine the factors that hindered the growth of nationalism in Germany, allowing pupils to judge the main obstacle or obstacles to the growth of nationalism.

Background

As we have discussed in the previous two chapters, the period of 1815 to 1850 in Germany was one of growing nationalism. Economic, cultural and military factors all encouraged a growth of nationalist ideas. Events such as the French Revolution and the dissolution of the Holy Roman Empire contributed to the increasing number of Germans calling for a united Germany. As discussed in Chapter 2, there was strong support for a united Germany, especially among the **liberals** and educated middle class. The achievements of the Frankfurt Parliament and lasting impacts of the 1848 revolution suggest that there had been a significant growth of nationalist thought. However, there are also limitations to the idea that nationalism had grown to a significant extent. The concept of a united Germany had powerful opponents, such as **conservative** Austria and Prussia, and there was a lack of active support among the peasants. Ultimately, the nationalist hopes of German unification in 1850 seemed a long way off.

This chapter discusses the obstacles to German unification, allowing you to evaluate the relative importance of each. We will discuss the divisions among nationalists, be it in their ideas of or approach to achieving a united Germany. We will also focus on the power of Austria, particularly in relation to the role played by the chancellor Klemens von Metternich and the Austrian humiliation of the Prussians at Olmütz. This chapter will also highlight the particularism of the German states and show the reluctance of many of the ruling princes to relinquish their own **sovereignty** in a united Germany.

Finally, we will examine the indifference of many in Germany to unification, such as the peasants, whose concerns were of a more immediate **socioeconomic** nature, rather than focused on high politics.

As before, it is important to note that the content in this chapter has significant overlap with previous chapters. This is intentional, as it follows the themes set out in the examination. You may use the information from previous chapters to respond to the question of evaluating the obstacles to German unification. However, you must be aware that if you take this approach, be sure to always link the evidence to the question that is being asked in the examination.

3.1 What obstacles were there to German unification?

For the purposes of the examination, it is important to be able to evaluate the factors that hindered German unification. This chapter sets out the main obstacles to German unification and supports candidates in evaluating the relative importance of these obstacles.

This section will examine the following factors:

| Divisions among the nationalists |
| Austrian strength |
| German princes |
| Religious differences |
| Indifference of the masses |

Understanding these issues will allow you to make a judgement on the main obstacle or obstacles to German unification, 1815–50.

3.1.1 Divisions among the nationalists

While it is fair to argue that there had been a growth of nationalist ideas among many Germans, nationalists were divided over what a united Germany would look like, as well as how to achieve it.

Differences of ideas

One of the issues dividing nationalists was that there were two competing ideas about what shape a unified Germany should take. Some argued the territorial extent should include nearly all German speakers, taking in significant parts of Austria. Others felt it would be more practical to create a lesser Germany, excluding Austria but including all of Prussia. These differences among nationalists became a major obstacle to the creation of a united Germany.

The first, and arguably most popular, model was to form a so-called **Grossdeutschland**. Given that so much cultural nationalism had focused on the **primordial** nature of the German **Volk** and their need to live in a common **nation-state**, the initial position was that this should define the nature of a new, united Germany. Grossdeutschland would include not only the 39 German states but also the predominantly German-speaking regions of the Austrian Empire. The alternative was to form a lesser Germany, or **Kleindeutschland**. Less ambitious in scope, this plan would create a united Germany that excluded Austria but contained each of the 39 German states. It would also include and be dominated by Prussia.

In October 1848, the Frankfurt Parliament voted for the Grossdeutschland model. However, under the leadership of new conservative prime minister Prince Felix of Schwarzenberg (1848–52), Austria refused to allow it and declared the Austrian Empire indivisible. After heated debates, moderate proponents of the Kleindeutschland solution, led by liberal Heinrich von Gagern, came to dominate.

Figure 3.1 Prince Felix of Schwarzenberg, the conservative prime minister of Austria, strove to restore Austrian power in the wake of the 1848 revolution. His policies were similar to those of his predecessor, Metternich

This issue of the future territorial extent of Germany was a key division among nationalists and an important obstacle to the unification of Germany. With little agreement and powerful opposition from Austria, this made it harder to build **consensus** and act decisively to unify Germany. The issue also dominated the early proceedings of the Frankfurt Parliament and delayed the progress of important constitutional matters during the political vacuum that had been created in early 1848. This was a major challenge to the operation of the embattled Frankfurt Parliament and highlighted that if nationalists were going to progress the idea of a united Germany, they had significant differences to resolve first.

Division between liberals and radicals

In addition, those Germans calling for unity were divided over the nature of a united Germany.

Liberal Germans were in favour of a **constitutional monarchy**. This would create a political union between all the German states, protect the rights of individuals and create a parliament that would be the primary source of law. All of this would be presided over by a constitutional monarch. This system would establish a political system close in nature to that of Britain at the time. Liberals were almost exclusively well-educated and established members of the middle class. They had been inspired by the cultural writings and ideas of the Romantic and nationalist movements. Yet although they wanted reform, they saw this primarily as an evolution of the German states, rather than a revolution. Indeed, middle-class liberals were passionately opposed to revolution, fearful of repeating the violent excesses seen during the terror of the French Revolution.

The other main group calling for a united Germany, the radicals, were aware of the emerging theories on capitalism, such as *The Communist Manifesto*, written by Karl Marx and Friedrich Engels in 1848, which summarised many of the widely existing sentiments of the period.

Figure 3.2 Karl Marx was a German historian, economist and revolutionary. He argued that history was defined by a series of class conflicts which would bring about the social system of communism. His ideas were particularly attractive to urban workers

Despite wanting many of the same changes as liberals were calling for, radical Germans believed the reforms should go even further. They viewed the reforms proposed by the liberals as positive for the middle class, but less so for the urban working class. They therefore called for more **revolutionary** change, including the abolition of the monarchy and the granting of a universal male franchise. And they were active in seeking this change. For example, in September 1848 a group of radical Germans stormed the Paulskirche where the Frankfurt Parliament was meeting. Though troops were defending those gathered, around 80 people were killed, including two conservative deputies. In response, martial law was declared.

However, the radicals were unwilling to give up, and in October they denounced the Frankfurt Parliament as only representing middle- and upper-class Germans. They declared the parliament illegitimate and called for new elections.

This was a significant obstacle to German unification, as it not only divided those calling for a united Germany, but encouraged liberals to adopt a more conservative position through their fear of revolution. Had liberals and radicals been able to cooperate to achieve a united Germany, it would have made proceedings in the Frankfurt Parliament far easier. Instead, these two pro-unification groups were bitterly divided. Moreover, the actions of the radicals slowed the work of the Frankfurt Parliament, leaving it less able to advance the political argument for a united Germany. Therefore, the divisions among nationalists were a significant barrier to German unification.

On the other hand…

There were cases when nationalists were able to cooperate and put aside their fundamental differences in order to enact decrees which advanced the cause of German nationalism. For example, nationalists cooperated to enact the Fifty Articles in the autumn of 1848. This unexpected achievement brought equality before the law, individual freedoms and an end to class discrimination. There was also agreement on the nature of the German Constitution by March 1849. Although the agreement only passed by 267 votes to 263, it showed that there was perhaps sufficient momentum to advance the cause of a united Germany. It also demonstrated that proponents of nationalism were not so divided that they could not make key decisions. This limits the argument that divisions among nationalists were the main obstacle to a united Germany.

The historian M. Fulbrook outlines some of the successes of the Frankfurt Parliament (Source 1), pointing out what was achieved when radicals and liberals cooperated.

> ### SOURCE 1
>
> Agreement was finally hammered out or cobbled together on certain issues. Individualistic economic policies and freedom of trade were supported; a doctrine of fundamental rights was published on 28 December 1848; it was agreed that a united Germany should be a federal state with an emperor and an elected parliament responsible to the ministry; and, after considerable bargaining … there was an unexpected vote for almost universal manhood suffrage on 29 April 1849.
>
> **Fulbrook, M. (2019)** *A Concise History of Germany* **(3rd edn), Cambridge University Press**

Overall

While there were important times when nationalists worked together, such as in the passing of the Fifty Articles in 1848 and the German Constitution in 1849, clearly there was a significant divide among those Germans calling for a united Germany. The disruption caused during the sitting of the Frankfurt Parliament is proof of the divide among nationalists and the negative impact of radical actions on the business of Germany's first parliament. Indeed, M. Fulbrook argues that 'on certain major substantive issues there proved to be insurmountable problems'. This suggests that the divisions among nationalists were a significant barrier to the creation of a united Germany.

3.1.2 Austrian strength

Another significant obstacle to the unification of Germany was Austrian strength. Although during the period of 1815–50 Prussia had become more economically powerful, Austria remained militarily and politically dominant. Given that Austria was deeply conservative and implacably opposed to the idea of a united Germany, this was a powerful obstacle to German unification.

The role of Metternich

As we have previously discussed, many historians argue that nationalism was on the rise in the German states between 1815 and 1850. Evidence of this can be found in the emergence of nationalist student fraternities and gymnastic groups which called for a united Germany. They were inspired by cultural and literary developments that classified a relatively new type of ethnic nationalism, which identified the German Volk as a primordial people, unique in their preservation of language and history. These thinkers, students and university lecturers argued that the German Volk should live within a united German nation-state, the **Vaterland**. These ideas were seen in Austria as a direct threat to the empire's power, and as such were shut down quickly.

The architect for the suppression of the growth of German nationalism was Klemens von Metternich, Austria's foreign minister and chancellor. He was deeply **reactionary**, and opposed the growth of democracy and nationalism, both of which he felt threatened Austria's position as the head of an ethnically diverse empire and dominant political force in central Europe.

In response to the growth of nationalism among the educated middle class, Metternich introduced the Carlsbad Decrees in 1819. These were accepted by the Bundestag and introduced significant restrictions to individual freedoms. The decrees enforced the disbanding of student societies, ushered in press censorship and inspectors for universities, and threatened radical university lecturers with dismissal. These were reinforced in 1832 when Metternich, with Prussian support, passed the Six Articles in response to nationalist festivals, such as the one at Hambach (see page 8). The Six Articles strengthened the suppression of nationalism, even formalising the use of troops to crush any nationalist gatherings.

The historian A. Farmer sets out some of the details of the articles (Source 2).

SOURCE 2

[The Six Articles] increased the Bundestag's control over the internal affairs of individual states, and, in particular, its control of the universities and the press. The Bundestag's member states agreed to send military assistance to any government threatened by unrest.

Farmer, A. (2020) *Access to History: The Unification of Germany and the Challenge of Nationalism 1789–1919*, **Hodder Education**

This was strengthened yet further in 1834, when Metternich summoned members of the German Confederation to meet in Vienna. There he set out a system of even greater censorship and control, with agreement from all members of the Bundestag.

These events demonstrate how Metternich and the Austrians were a major obstacle to German unification. Not only did their actions shut down the early growth of nationalism in the German states but they also revealed how the Bundestag was little more than a political tool of Austria. It was clear that Metternich was able to dictate to the delegates of the 39 states how they should act, even in relation to internal affairs. Austrian conservatism and dominance was, therefore, a significant barrier to a united Germany.

Events at Olmütz

In the wake of the 1848 revolution, the system of the German Confederation had been cast aside in favour of a national parliament. This parliament sat in Frankfurt, and by 1849 had agreed to a German Constitution. Although the Prussian king, Frederick William IV, had refused to accept parliament's offer to make him emperor of a united Germany, the idea began to appeal to him more and more. He came to accept the notion of unification with the Prussian king acting as German emperor, provided that all states agreed to this plan.

By March 1850, a new Reich had been formed, comprised of 28 German states. The group included powerful states such as Hannover and Saxony and held a parliament in Erfurt.

Figure 3.3 The so-called Erfurt Parliament met in a monastery in Erfurt, in central Germany. The Austrian government acted swiftly to counter any growth in nationalist sentiment by forcing the Prussians and other states to disband this fledgling political institution

This action was met with intense hostility by Austria. The new Austrian chancellor, Schwarzenberg, believed this was an attempt by Prussia to increase its political power at the expense of Austria's. Initially, the Austrians were too preoccupied with the fallout of the 1848 revolution to be able to act. However, as the Austrian **counter-revolution** restored traditional power, the Austrians called the 39 delegates of the old German Confederation to meet in Frankfurt in May 1850. This caused immediate tension, as now there were two bodies claiming to speak for Germany: the Prussian-dominated Erfurt Union and the Austrian-dominated German Confederation.

In November 1850, leaders from both sides arranged to meet at Olmütz, in the modern-day Czech Republic. There the Prussians agreed to abandon their political union and formally re-establish the old German Confederation of 1815 in which Austria was dominant.

This was a humiliating defeat for the Prussians and a diplomatic victory for the Austrians. It thwarted Prussia's attempts to forge a political German union that excluded Austria. It also allowed Austria to undo most of the political progress made in Germany in 1848 and 1849 and revert to the old political system. This infuriated many Germans, particularly Prussians, who were becoming increasingly determined to create a Prussian-dominated, united Germany. However, in 1850 Austria clearly stood in the way. Therefore, it seems fair to argue that Austria was a significant obstacle to the unification of Germany in 1850.

On the other hand…

While the Austrians had secured a major political victory at Olmütz, it was also clear that their ability to challenge Prussia economically was waning. For example, in 1849, Chancellor Schwarzenberg attempted to establish a **customs union** that would compete with the powerful **Zollverein**. However, the proposed Zollunion failed, and in combination with the growing expense of maintaining military garrisons to preserve order in the wake of the 1848 revolution, it could be said that Austria's ability to influence German politics was declining. This perhaps limits the argument that Austrian power was the main obstacle to the unification of Germany.

Overall

Nonetheless, it remains clear that Austria was fundamentally opposed to the idea of a united Germany. Metternich was active in his suppression of nationalist ideas, and although he was forced to flee to London during the 1848 revolution, his successor was equally opposed to the idea of a united Germany.

As Austria regained control following the disruptions of 1848–49, it remained a powerful block to the creation of a German nation-state. While economically Austria was arguably losing ground to the powerful German economic union, the Austrians were able to maintain their political dominance over the German states, as demonstrated by the Treaty of Olmütz. Therefore, it seems fair to state that Austrian strength remained a significant block to German unification by 1850.

3.1.3 German princes

Another barrier to the unification of Germany was the German princes themselves. These rulers were sovereign in their own states, and so were often reluctant to give up their power in favour of a united Germany, likely under the dominance of Prussia.

Particularism

After the political system was reformed in 1815, there were 39 German states. Each state had its own history, traditions and culture. While they shared the same language, albeit with strong regional dialects, there was a sense of individual peculiarity between states. This was born out of the preceding Holy Roman Empire, during which there existed hundreds of states within the borders of modern-day Germany. They differed religiously, politically and economically – the north and east of Germany were mostly agrarian and authoritarian, with significant pockets of industrialisation, especially in the Ruhr district and Berlin, while the south and west were primarily industrial and more liberal.

This was a barrier to unification as not only were state rulers unwilling to sacrifice their hereditary power in the name of a united Germany, but many state citizens were also reticent to be subsumed into a larger, single political body, especially as such a Germany would likely be dominated by the powerful Prussia.

Lack of cooperation

The lack of willingness of the German princes to cooperate was often on display in the Frankfurt Parliament. Several princes merely tolerated the parliament's work – they felt they had no option, given the political turmoil of the 1840s. Their reluctance was clear to see when it came to the suppression of nationalism in the wake of the 1848 revolution. For example, in 1849 there were major uprisings in favour of the constitution that had been drawn up by the Frankfurt Parliament. However, German princes were willing to use military violence to crush any opposition to the status quo. Rather than accept a Prussian imposition, the Baden and Saxony princes themselves, for example, called in Prussian troops to crush nationalist uprisings.

This shows that the princes' lack of eagerness to cooperate was a major block to unification. Many princes appeared determined to hold on to their regional authority rather than accept a single central power, even to the point of being willing to deploy troops and weapons to crush challenges to their power.

On the other hand…

One could argue that the strength of regional particularism was waning by 1850. This was primarily driven by the growth of interconnected transport networks, spurred on by the success of economic integration. Roads, canals and, crucially, rail networks connected German states that had been hitherto isolated and insular. This allowed for the spread of increasingly popular literature, pamphlets and ideas. This limits the argument that particularism and local traditions and customs were a significant obstacle to the unification of Germany.

Overall

It seems fair to argue that regional particularism and the German princes provided a significant block to the unification of Germany. Clearly the rulers of many German states wanted to retain absolute authority rather than ceding power to a united Germany of equal members. Indeed, that the princes were willing to relinquish all nationalist progress in the face of the humiliating defeat at Olmütz suggests they were satisfied to accept Austrian domination if it meant they retained their own power and authority.

3.1.4 Religious differences

As the philosopher Kant states: 'Nature employs two means to separate peoples … differences of language and of religion.' Historically, German states were so divided in terms of religion, it may have made the realisation of a united Germany much harder to achieve.

The historian H. W. Smith highlights this in Source 3:

SOURCE 3

Nations depend on a certain amount of fellow feeling, on a sense, however contrived, that fellow citizens represent kith and kin. Typically this sense derives from a common history, a common memory. Yet while that memory may evoke heroic acts and legendary figures of the distant past, it may also recall civil war and religious intolerance, hatred, and persecution, betrayal and subterfuge.

Smith, H. W. (1995) *German Nationalism and Religious Conflict: Culture, Ideology, Politics 1870–1914*, **Princeton University Press**

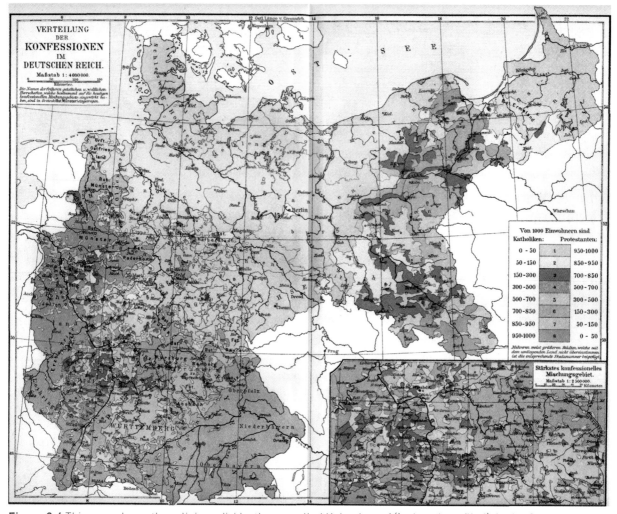

Figure 3.4 This map shows the religious divide, the so-called Kulturkampf ('cultural conflict'), in the German states around this time. This division was a major obstacle to unification

Differences between northern and southern Germany

Broadly speaking, nineteenth-century Germany was divided into the Protestant north and east, and the Catholic south and west. As historian T. Nipperdey highlighted, while there was a degree of 'cooperation and coexistence … [religious] division and tension was one of the fundamental, vital facts of everyday life in Germany'. Recent events remained powerful reminders of the division. The nineteenth-century German Catholics would certainly remember when German Protestants destroyed the great *Una Sancta* ('church unity') of the Holy Roman Empire. Conversely, Protestant Germans saw Catholicism as a source of intolerance which stirred up acts of violence, such as the massacre of the Protestant population by Count von Tilly's armies during the Sack of Magdeburg on 20 May 1631. The division between Protestant and Catholic was so stark that popular writers, such as the folklorist Wilhelm Heinrich Riehl, found it necessary to adapt their works to suit either Protestant or Catholic audiences.

Therefore, there existed a massive cultural rift between the north and the south. That the cultural memory of many Germans was one of mistrust, fear or even loathing of members of the opposing religion clearly made it significantly harder to achieve a united Germany by 1850.

On the other hand…

Despite these differences, the work of the Frankfurt Parliament showed that agreement was possible, despite religious differences. Indeed, many of the political decisions made by the parliament were divided along class lines, for example liberal versus radical, rather than religious. This suggests that religious divides may not have been the main obstacle to German unification.

Overall

Religious divides did, in many ways, drive a wedge between north and east Germany, and the south and west. The Protestant and Catholic divide was stark, and each community pointed to the failures and injustices of the other, making it harder to achieve both cultural and political unity. In effect, the German nation was divided, challenging the idea of a united Volk.

3.1.5 Indifference of the masses

A final obstacle to the unification of Germany is the existence of groups within the German states who did not necessarily oppose nationalism but were also not interested in pursuing it. This lack of active support for the idea of a united Germany was, in effect, a barrier to unification.

Lack of peasant support

During the 1840s, German peasants endured great hardship. The majority lived and worked in rural areas, where the socioeconomic problems of the mid-nineteenth century were most acutely felt. As we saw earlier, Germany's population had doubled since the mid-eighteenth century, which placed huge pressure on food production. They also faced the effects of a severe potato famine. Together, these crises left the majority of German peasants landless and made them victims of feudal injustices, forcing them into extreme poverty.

It is clear that by the 1840s some peasants blamed the political system for their plight. The confederation of 39 states, with its mostly disconnected infrastructures, economies and agricultural practices, led to highly inefficient systems of food production and distribution. Moreover, landowning classes, such as the **Junkers** in Prussia, had extreme powers over the peasants who worked their lands. However, despite the extreme hardships, most peasants did not view the creation of a united Germany, which could help to solve their problems, as a major concern.

One reason for this was that much of the nationalistic literature being produced around this time was not designed with the peasantry in mind. Although literacy rates were improving in Germany in the mid-nineteenth century, there remained many illiterate peasants. This precluded them from accessing the resources that thinkers, poets and philosophers were producing.

Moreover, although a reform and rationalisation of the disparate state economies might have eventually led to an improvement in the living and working conditions of rural peasants, to many this seemed a long way off. The peasantry had more immediate socioeconomic concerns – avoiding starvation was far more pressing than the intellectual notion of a German Vaterland.

In addition, the peasantry went unrepresented in the so-called 'Professors' Parliament'. Many rural workers were convinced that parliaments such as Frankfurt would have no bearing on their lives and would seek only to better the political representation of the educated middle class. Consequently, there was very little support among the peasantry for the idea of a united Germany, which in itself was a significant obstacle to unification.

On the other hand…

It is clear that the peasantry was not happy with the status quo, particularly when it came to the feudal powers and rights the landed aristocracy held over rural workers. Therefore, if a united Germany could have been a vehicle for introducing broad reform to rural regions, then they might have been broadly sympathetic to such an idea.

Overall

It seems clear that there was a great deal of apathy in the rural regions to the idea of a united Germany, especially in 1847–48 when there were better-than-average harvests. As the economic situation of the peasantry improved, calls for reform decreased, suggesting their apathy was a significant barrier to unification. Had the idea of a united Germany been attractive to the peasants, then it would certainly have been far more likely to succeed. The fact that the peasants cared most about their own conditions was clear to see following many of the reforms brought in by rulers in the wake of the 1848 revolution. For example, most states eased or eliminated the authoritarian control of feudalism in 1848–49, which appeared to satisfy the peasantry in the short term. Indeed, many peasants felt animosity towards rather than an affinity with educated nationalists, providing a further obstacle to unification.

What was the main obstacle to the growth of nationalism in Germany?

Though nationalism was on the increase in Germany, it is clear that there were many obstacles to unification. First, the division among nationalists proved tricky, with those in favour of a united Germany split on what form it should take. Second, there was strong resistance from Austria to the idea of a united Germany. The Austrians were able to exploit the divisions within Germany, be they religious or cultural, and politically limit any moves towards unification. Combined with the indifference of many groups of Germans, such as the peasantry, to support a united Germany, it is clear that there were many powerful obstacles to this concept.

ACTIVITIES

1 Create a political spectrum.
  a) Draw a horizontal line on a blank piece of paper.
  b) Write 'left wing' on the far left, and 'right wing' on the far right.
  c) Position the following terms in the appropriate position along the line:
    • reactionary
    • conservative
    • liberal
    • radical
  d) Beneath each of these terms, write two to three sentences describing the members of the group. Include information such as who they were, what they wanted and their views on a united Germany.

2 Create a visual diagram detailing the obstacles to the unification of Germany.
   a) Draw a vertical line.
   b) Place each of the five main obstacles listed within this chapter on the line. The most significant obstacle should be positioned at the top, the least at the bottom. Place the other factors on the line in descending order of importance.
   c) Write two to three sentences to justify why you have chosen the factor at the top of the line as the most important.
   d) Justify why each other factor is less important than the top factor.

3 Explain how Klemens von Metternich and Austria could limit the growth of nationalism in Germany. Do this in two to three sentences. Repeat this for each of the other four factors.

4 Create a large mind map showing all of the barriers to German unification.
   a) Write 'obstacles to unification' in the centre.
   b) Write each of the five factors as 'legs'.
   c) Include at least three pieces of knowledge in support of each factor.

GLOSSARY

Term	Meaning
consensus	General agreement on a matter.
conservative	Someone averse to change or who holds traditional values.
constitutional monarchy	System of government in which the monarch shares authority with a constitutionally organised government.
counter-revolution	A revolution that is intended to reverse the effects of a previous revolution.
customs union	A group of participants (states, countries etc.) that agree to reduce or eliminate taxes to enable the free movement of goods between members.
Grossdeutschland	Greater Germany, which would unify all German-speaking people (including those in parts of Austria) under one state.
Junker	A Prussian noble or aristocrat.
Kleindeutschland	Lesser Germany, which would create a united Germany that excluded Austria but contained each of the 39 German states.
liberal	Relating to or denoting a political and social philosophy that promotes individual rights, civil liberties, democracy and free enterprise.
nation-state	A sovereign state in which most of the citizens or subjects are united by factors that define a nation, such as language or common descent.
primordial	Existing since the beginning of time.
reactionary	Someone who opposes political or social progress or reform.
revolutionary	Someone engaged in political revolution or dramatic change.
socioeconomic	A measure of social standing based on social and economic factors.
sovereignty	Supreme power or authority.
Vaterland	Fatherland. The land from which one originates.
Volk	The German people.
Zollverein	A customs union of German states formed to manage tariffs and economic policies. It was created by the 1833 Zollverein treaties and formally started on 1 January 1834.

Chapter 4

An evaluation of the reasons why unification was achieved in Germany by 1871

The aim of this chapter is to evaluate the reasons why Germany was eventually unified in 1871.

Background

As discussed in the previous three chapters, nationalism had been growing in the German states up to 1850, although mostly among the educated middle-class and liberal Germans. However, after the failure of the 1848 revolution to deliver a united Germany and the Prussian humiliation at Olmütz in 1850, it appeared that unification was a long way off. Yet, within 21 years of Olmütz, Germany was a united country under Prussian leadership. The question is, how was this possible?

When discussing the unification of Germany, it is important to frame it correctly. It was not so much a coming together of equal German states to create a democratic and popular German government but rather an increasingly dominant Prussia forging a united Germany under its leadership.

The historian L. Abrams explains the situation in Source 1.

SOURCE 1

In 1848 there had been little evidence of popular or grass-roots nationalist sentiment and despite the emergence of nationalist association and the spread of education, which promoted a greater sense of cultural and linguistic unity, the same was true in 1871 when the German lands were ultimately unified. The German question was resolved not by speeches and majority verdicts favoured by the liberals, but by blood and iron as Bismarck had predicted in 1862. In practice, unification can legitimately be seen as a form of Prussian expansionism.

Abrams, L. (1995) *Bismarck and the German Empire, 1871–1918,* **Routledge**

In effect, Germany was able to become a united country through the Prussians winning a series of short wars, which removed all obstacles to the creation of a united Germany dominated by Prussia. The Prussians defeated the Danes in 1864, the Austrians during the Austro-Prussian War (or Seven Weeks' War) of 1866, and the French in the Franco-Prussian War of 1870–71. Therefore, much of the discussion of this chapter revolves around this growing Prussian strength. We will discuss this both in **real terms** and also compare it to neighbouring countries, particularly France and Austria.

Additionally, this chapter will discuss the role of Otto von Bismarck, who rose from being a relatively unimportant Prussian **Junker** to, some would argue, the architect of German unification and Prussian dominance.

Figure 4.1 An engraving of Bismarck from 1870. His role has been hotly debated by historians, though it appears that in many ways his actions and decisions contributed to the unification of Germany

Finally, we will discuss the role of other countries – both the comparative strength of Prussia and also in relation to the willingness of Britain and Russia to accept an emerging Prussia as the dominant force in central Europe.

Taken together, this discussion will allow you to argue what the main factor or factors were that led to German unification in 1871.

4.1 Why was unification achieved in 1871?

For the purposes of the examination, it is important to be able to evaluate the reasons that led to German unification in 1871. This chapter sets out the key events and allows you to come to a conclusion about what the main factor or factors were that ultimately led to unification.

This section will examine the following factors:

Prussian military strength
Prussian economic strength
The decline of Austria
Role of Bismarck
Role of other countries

Understanding these issues will allow you to make a judgement on the main reason, or reasons, why Germany united in 1871.

4.1.1 Prussian military strength

The Prussian military was central to the concept of the unification of Germany. Indeed, Prussian military victories over neighbouring France and Austria allowed Germany to become united under Prussian leadership.

Prussia had introduced a range of social and economic reforms in the wake of defeats during the Napoleonic Wars. These included improvements to education and the abolition of feudal practices which were holding back the process of industrialisation. By the 1860s Prussia was looking to replicate these forward-thinking policies within its military, and in so doing create an army that was arguably better led, equipped and trained than that of any neighbouring state. It was perhaps the creation of this army that is the main reason behind the forging of a united Germany in 1871.

Nature of the Prussian army

Although Prussian economic strength had steadily been improving throughout the first half of the nineteenth century, some Prussians voiced concerns about the state and strength of the Prussian army. King William I of Prussia was worried about the condition of the Prussian army and was well aware that no real army reform had taken place since 1815. It was becoming clear to the king and the army's general staff that the troops were neither well equipped nor prepared for speedy **mobilisation** and deployment. This meant the army would be less able to protect and advance Prussia's interests in Germany and beyond.

To resolve the situation, in 1860 the conservative army officer General von Roon introduced a bill that was designed to modernise the Prussian army by doubling its size, increasing the period of compulsory military service from two to three years, re-equipping the army with modern weapons and reducing the role played by the irregular **Landwehr** forces. However, the bill was initially unpopular among liberal Germans, who were concerned by the focus on military development, although they were unable to halt proceedings. As a result, the Prussian army grew quickly in size, and comprised more of professional soldiers rather than irregular volunteers.

By 1870, the army was 319,000 strong – significantly larger than, for example, Austria's army of 252,000. Additionally, it was equipped with new weapons which were far more effective than those that had come before. For example, old-fashioned muskets that could only fire a few bullets every minute were replaced with modern breech-loading guns which could fire five times faster.

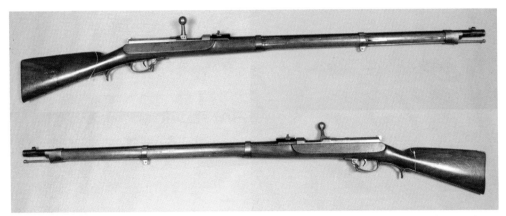

Figure 4.2 These rifles had a modern bolt-loading function, making them able to fire much faster than old-fashioned muskets. Modern weapons like these played a major role in Prussia's defeat of the armies of neighbouring states

The Prussian army was now large, professional and well equipped, enabling it to both challenge the military might of Prussia's neighbours and unite Germany. For example, in 1866, the Prussians defeated Austrian forces at the Battle of Sadowa. Although in terms of numbers the Prussian and Austrian forces were balanced, Prussian training and weaponry proved decisive. Not only did Prussian forces win this key battle but they also suffered 9,000 casualties to Austria's 45,000. This demonstrates how effective and decisive the Prussian army had become, and how instrumental it was to the unification of Germany.

Leadership

The Prussian army was not only increasingly professional and well equipped but also well led. During the conflicts with Austria and France, the military leadership of the generals von Roon and von Moltke contributed to Prussian victory, paving the way for the possible unification of Germany in 1871.

One way in which leadership proved effective was in military planning. In the mid-nineteenth century armies were often very large, even hundreds of thousands strong. Troops needed to be mobilised and transported to the areas of conflict, a task the Prussian generals were particularly adept at organising. For example, during the Austro-Prussian War (or Seven Weeks' War) of 1866, the Prussian field marshal Helmuth von Moltke picked the perfect time and place to attack the Austrian forces, which were spread out across Austria's large empire. He also chose a location that was connected to only one Austrian rail line, but five Prussian lines. This allowed Moltke to quickly deploy the large and modern Prussian army to battle, which caught the Austrians off guard. Similar tactics were employed during the Franco-Prussian War of 1870–71 when the Prussian-led German army attacked near Alsace-Lorraine, which was connected to five Prussian rail lines versus France's two.

Figure 4.3 General von Moltke has been described as a military genius. His leadership played a major role in Prussian military victories and, therefore, eventual German unification

Prussian generals were also skilled in the use of modern communication technology, such as the telegraph, to coordinate troops that were spread out. This contributed to German victory as it meant the Prussian army, often smaller or equal in size to its opponents, was able to take advantage of key technological advances in order to better concentrate its forces in one place. This enabled the Prussian army to quickly defeat opponents in Denmark, Austria and France, which helped pave the way for German unification in 1871.

On the other hand…

Though modern, professional and well equipped, the Prussian army was not invincible. Indeed, Moltke took great risks when deploying his forces to face the might of the Austrian army in 1866. He made the risky decision to divide his forces while he mobilised troops to concentrate the attack in the Bohemia region. Rather than its own strength, then, perhaps Prussian success can be ascribed to the failure of the Austrian generals to react, which limits the importance of Prussian military strength as an overall factor in Germany's unification.

Overall

It is clear that the growing strength and power of the Prussian army was central to the unification of Germany in 1871. The army was becoming better trained and equipped. For example, by the time the Prussian-German army challenged the French in 1871, it had created even more powerful cavalry divisions, replaced its old artillery with new, fast-loading weapons and extended Prussian military organisation to neighbouring German states. This modernisation, combined with highly effective military leadership and mobilisation strategies, allowed the Prussian army to defeat all other neighbouring states, which set Germany on its path to unification.

4.1.2 Prussian economic strength

Prussia was developing not only as a dominant military force within central Europe, but as an economic power too. This allowed Prussia to take a position of leadership among the German states, but also to challenge the economic power of neighbouring countries such as Austria and even France.

The historian A. Farmer sums up the economic advantage that Prussia enjoyed.

> **SOURCE 2**
>
> Prussian economic growth in the 1850s and 1860s outstripped that of Austria and France singly. By the mid-1860s, Prussia produced more coal and steel than France or Austria and had a more extensive railway network. In 1865 it possessed 15,000 steam engines with a total horsepower of 800,000. Austria, by contrast, had 3,400 steam engines with a total horsepower of 100,000. The economic and financial strength of Prussia provided it with the military resources it needed to challenge first Austria and then France. A key industrialist was Alfred Krupp, whose iron foundries in the Ruhr produced high-quality armaments.
>
> **Farmer, A. (2020)** *Access to History: The Unification of Germany and the Challenge of Nationalism 1789–1919* **(5th edn), Hodder Education**

During the mid-nineteenth century the German states were industrialising quickly. Coal, iron and textile production were booming, and railway lines in the German states doubled in length between 1850 and 1870. Prussia was at the forefront of the development, and one could argue that the economic advantages Prussia enjoyed enabled it to defeat neighbouring countries such as France and Austria, providing a route to state unification under Prussian leadership in 1871.

Nature of the Prussian economy

It is clear that the Prussian economy was growing quickly in the mid-nineteenth century. This has been attributed to several factors, including the rich supply of coal, access to iron ore and other raw materials, and state investment in the rapid building of railways. Several large industrial centres emerged in Germany in this period. These became a symbol for the success of Prussian industrialisation. For example, the Krupp Works in Essen employed thousands of workers by 1866, as well as producing modern weaponry for the Prussian army. This development was brought about by reforms both in rural regions and in cities that not only facilitated urbanisation and industrialisation but also provided a minimum standard of living for urban workers. Minimum wage levels for workers were encouraged, child labour was forbidden in factories, and inspectors and courts were set up to represent workers.

Moreover, Prussia continued to lead the **Zollverein**, which enabled the Prussian economy to benefit from the smaller markets of the other German states. This meant that the Prussian economy could grow quickly and stably. By 1870 the Prussian economy was highly developed and industrialised. The state grew wealthy, enabling it to pursue its plans to unite Germany under its own leadership, and equip the army with modern, decisive weapons. Taken together, this allowed the Prussian state to become even more powerful, facilitating the unification of Germany in 1871.

Comparative strength of the Prussian economy

The Prussian economy was growing not only in real terms but also in relation to states such as Austria. While the Prussian economy was developing and industrialising, the Austrian economy was stagnant. It remained primarily agricultural, and only pockets of western Austria were industrialising. Moreover, Austria was slow to develop its all-important rail network. For example, in 1870 Prussia operated 18,876 km of rail compared with just 9,589 km in Austria. Prussia's rapid development of its rail network even compared favourably to France, which in 1870 operated only 15,544km of rail. Combined with the fact that, in 1860, Prussia alone contributed 4.9 per cent to world manufacturing input, versus Austria's 4.2 per cent, we can clearly see how strong the Prussian economy was in relation to neighbouring states.

This was central to the unification of Germany, as it cemented Prussian economic dominance over the other German states. It allowed Prussia to challenge the leadership of other states, and particularly Austria, which had for so long dominated the German Confederation. With the balance of power tipping in Prussia's favour, the state was able to challenge Austria's historically dominant position and push for a united Germany under its leadership.

On the other hand…

Much has been made about the role and importance of the Zollverein in bringing about German unification in 1871. However, although clearly the Prussian customs union helped to boost the Prussian economy, this did not automatically lead to greater political unity. In fact many German states, particularly those in the south, still looked to Austria for political leadership and as a counter-balance to Prussia's growing economic dominance. This was evident during the Austro-Prussian War, during which many German states sided with Austria over Prussia. This suggests that perhaps Prussian economic strength was, in fact, an obstacle to unification.

Overall

That being said, it is clear that Prussia was increasingly economically powerful, and that this was linked to its ability to unite Germany in 1871. The historian M. Fulbrook states that: 'The growing economic disparity between Prussia and Austria was an important factor in the eventual victory of Prussia over Austria'. Therefore, although Prussian economic dominance was arguably a divisive rather than unifying factor, it enabled Prussia to challenge and defeat opponents through economic and military might. This ultimately led to the creation of a united Germany in 1871, under Prussian leadership.

4.1.3 The decline of Austria

While Prussia's economic and military strength was on the increase, Austria's power was declining. It could be argued that Austria's inability to challenge Prussia's growing power and influence made the unification of Germany possible by 1871.

Economics and the challenge of regional nationalism

As discussed in the previous section, the Austrian economy was backward compared to Prussia's. Austria had been slow to industrialise and the majority of the empire still functioned with a largely rural, agrarian economy.

However, it was not only this economic weakness that caused a decline in Austrian power. Austria was also experiencing rising government expenditure as it became increasingly embroiled in regional conflicts, such as during the so-called Italian War of 1859.

The historian M. Fulbrook examines why (Source 3).

> **SOURCE 3**
>
> Economic growth in Prussia stood in stark contrast to the preponderantly stagnant economy of Austria, whose industrial growth centres of Vienna, Prague, and Bohemia generally were outweighed by the vast swathes of economically backward agricultural regions. Austria also had to devote a considerable portion of the budget to military expenditure to deal with troublesome situations in Italy and the Balkans.
>
> **Fulbrook, M. (2019)** *A Concise History of Germany* **(3rd edn), Cambridge University Press**

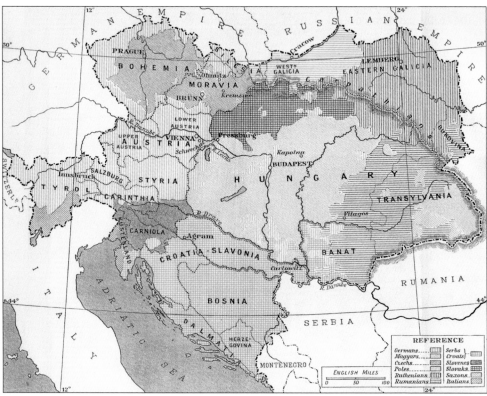

Figure 4.4 The Austrian Empire was home to a large mix of ethnic groups, including Czechs, Italians, Bosnians, Serbs, Hungarians, Poles, Ukrainians and Romanians, to name but a few.

Austria was faced with increasingly vociferous calls for regional autonomy within its empire. Moreover, it was forced to pay for large numbers of troops to be stationed throughout the empire to maintain order. This led to growing financial problems. Quite simply, the Austrian economy could not keep pace with neighbouring states.

This combination, of a slowly developing economy and the financial burden of stationing troops across a disparate empire, weakened Austria, lessening its ability to maintain its traditional dominance over German politics. It also struggled to maintain the conservative and reactionary anti-nationalist stance that had been such an obstacle to German unification between 1815 and 1850. Consequently, it could be argued that Austria's economic challenges became a contributing factor to the unification of Germany in 1871.

Isolated diplomatically

Austria had not only internal challenges but external ones too. Many of these were connected to Austria's increasingly isolated diplomatic position.

In 1853, an international alliance that included Britain, France and the Ottoman Empire defeated the Russian Empire during the Crimean War. Austria, though ostensibly remaining neutral, shifted tacit support between one side and the other. Though at times supporting Russia, Austria ended up siding with the British and French. This angered the Russians, and drove a wedge between Russia and Austria. Moreover, given that the Austrians gave only half-hearted support to the French and British, Austria did not gain support from them in return. This was arguably a foolish strategy and left Austria diplomatically isolated. The nation became further isolated in the wake of the Italian War of 1859, during which some Italian states, with French support, were successful in seceding from Austrian control. This was a further blow to Austrian prestige.

The decline of Austria was a significant reason why Germany was able to unite in 1871, as it allowed Prussia to challenge Austria as an isolated state rather than as a member of a powerful alliance. When Prussia declared war on Austria in 1866, powerful states like Britain, France and Russia chose to remain neutral, helping Prussia to victory and Germany to eventual unification.

Figure 4.5 This painting portrays the Prussian victory at the Battle of Sadowa in July 1866. Pictured at centre are the Prussian king William I, the brilliant General von Moltke, and Otto von Bismarck, for whom the battle was seen as a personal victory

On the other hand…

It is important not to overemphasise the decline of Austrian power. In 1866, Austria remained able to deploy significant military force to resist the designs of other states. For example, during the Austro-Prussian War, Austria deployed more soldiers than the Prussians did and had the support of many of the southern German states, including Bavaria. Moreover, Prussia's industrial advantages would not have had much of an impact on a short war. Plus, at the Battle of Sadowa in July 1866 Austrian artillery was initially very effective against the Prussians. This perhaps goes some way to limiting the argument that Austria's decline made German unification possible.

Overall

Although clearly not a spent force, Austria had evidently lost its ability to dictate the direction of German politics. The Austrian influence that was on display during the humiliation of Olmütz in 1850 must have felt like a distant memory by 1866, when an isolated Austria was quickly defeated by a superior Prussian force. The battle became a symbol of declining Austrian political and economic power and highlighted how diplomatically isolated Austria was. It seems fair to argue that this declining power played at least some role in the unification of Germany in 1871.

4.1.4 Role of Bismarck

During attempts to force through the army reforms of 1860, Prussia went through a constitutional crisis, as liberals and conservatives fought over who should hold the power in Prussia. It was during this crisis that the Prussian king William I appointed Otto von Bismarck – Junker, law graduate, civil servant and politician – as chief minister.

Bismarck's role in the unification of Germany remains controversial. For some, he was the near flawless architect of unification, while for others he was simply an opportunist who made the most of every situation he found himself in. Nevertheless, one could argue that it was his determination and diplomatic skill that led to Germany uniting in 1871.

Aim for Prussian domination

Bismarck was loyal, first and foremost, to Prussia. His actions as chief minister appear to have revolved around ensuring that Prussia would be the dominant power in a united Germany. He didn't take this position because a united Germany was desirable. Rather, he believed this was the surest way to maintain Prussian dominance over the other German states.

Bismarck's first speech to the Prussian Parliament, on 30 September 1862, made clear his aims and intentions (Source 4).

> **SOURCE 4**
>
> 'Germany is not looking to Prussia's liberalism, but to its power: Bavaria, Württemberg, Baden may indulge liberalism, but no one will expect them to take Prussia's role … to consolidate [German] strength … by iron and blood.'
>
> **Bismarck quoted in Medlicott, W. N. and Coveney, D. K. (1971) *Bismarck and Europe*, St Martin's Press**

Bismarck was a shrewd politician. He was opportunistic and logical when it came to making decisions. He realised, for instance, that conservative forces in Prussia would need to rely on popular support. Given that liberal and educated middle-class Prussians did not agree with his conservative politics, he quickly realised that he would have to compromise his principles in order to gain liberal support. He strove to strike a middle ground between liberals and conservatives. This approach came to be known as **realpolitik**, the politics of pragmatism rather than ideology. By adopting this approach Bismarck was able to retain his position within Prussia, and later a united Germany. Moreover, his decisive actions drew support from nationalist-minded liberals, who gave him their backing in the Prussian Parliament.

This support contributed to the unification of Germany in 1871, as it enabled Bismarck to act shrewdly in the interests of advancing the cause of a united Germany which would be dominated by Prussia. He was able to maintain stability and internal unity in Prussian politics, which allowed for a more powerful international projection of Prussian power. While some Prussians criticised Bismarck's political flexibility, most respected his judgement. This is most apparent in the fact that Bismarck maintained his position as chief adviser to the Prussian monarchy for almost 30 years.

Diplomacy

Perhaps the most dramatic example of Bismarck's influence on unification is his foreign policy. Bismarck initiated wars with Austria, Denmark and France, removing the final obstacles to a united Germany.

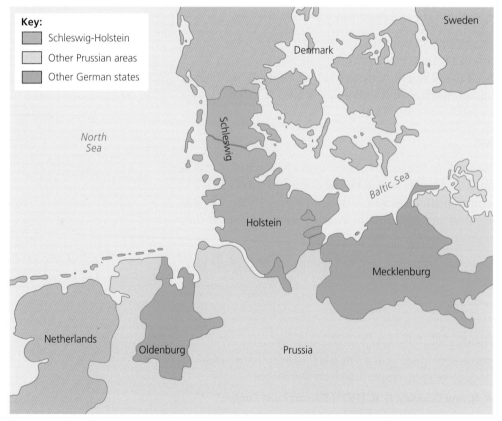

Figure 4.6 The Danish succession crisis and the opportunity it presented for Prussia to expand its power into other German states is a prime example of Bismarck's realpolitik

For example, Schleswig-Holstein had been under Danish control for nearly 400 years. However, the Danes sparked nationalist uproar in the German states when they formally tried to integrate the region into the Danish kingdom in 1848. Then, in 1863, the Danish king Frederick VII died childless. Denmark was facing a succession crisis, which was only resolved by placing Christian of Glucksburg (of the Duchy of Schleswig) on the throne. Christian was only eligible through his marriage to the late king's cousin. Although this move was accepted internationally, German nationals resisted, arguing that such an arrangement was illegal and that the Danes should pick their own ruler.

Bismarck acted decisively. He allied with Austria in defiance of Denmark and sent an **ultimatum** to the new Danish king, stating that if Danish forces did not withdraw from Schleswig-Holstein, Prussia would occupy the region. When the Danes refused to leave, the Prussian army marched into the area and defeated them. Battles such as those at the Danish fortifications of Duppel in April 1864 even earned Bismarck the support of reluctant liberals, who saw his actions as their best chance for achieving independence for Schleswig-Holstein and, ultimately, unification for Germany.

This was a significant step towards unification, as the victory won further land and resources for Prussia in northern Germany. It also demonstrated the power and force of the emerging Prussian army, with its superior military equipment. However, perhaps more importantly, Austria became embroiled in a fractious relationship with Prussia over what should be done with these regions. Some historians have argued that Bismarck intentionally created this tense relationship, so as to engineer a future war with Austria.

Bismarck realised that Austria was in decline, both economically and militarily, and that it was also diplomatically isolated. In a period of growing tension, he was able to forge a secret alliance with Italy against Austria, stoke tension over Schleswig-Holstein and challenge Austria in the **Bundestag**. In June 1866, Prussia left the German Confederation, declared it **dissolved** and demanded that north German states side with Prussia in a war against Austria. When they refused, they were quickly occupied and overrun by Prussian forces in advance of the so-called Seven Weeks' War.

This was a key step in the unification of Germany, as it enabled Prussia to further consolidate its control over northern Germany and remove Austrian influence from the majority of the German states. Moreover, the Treaty of Prague that ended the Seven Weeks' War, though not excessively punitive, allowed for the formation of a North German Confederation under Prussian leadership. This was a significant step towards the unification of Germany.

Bismarck was now ready to take his final steps towards the creation of a united Germany. He was reluctant to spark open warfare with France, which he viewed as significantly more powerful than either Austria or Denmark. However, although relations between the two remained peaceful, tensions began to rise.

For example, Bismarck expertly exploited a royal succession crisis in Spain. The Queen of Spain was forced to flee during the Spanish revolution of 1868. Her proposed replacement was a member of the Hohenzollern family. However, the French were strongly opposed to this, given that King William I of Prussia was the head of the Hohenzollern family, and they wanted to avoid being surrounded by potentially hostile monarchies.

Hoping to prevent a war, King William withdrew his son Leopold's candidacy, seemingly settling the issue. However, the French demanded a humiliating declaration from King William that Leopold would be excluded from the Spanish succession for 'all time'. Still hoping to avoid war, the Prussian king dictated a telegram for Bismarck to send to the French, which summarised a conversation between the king and the French ambassador. Bismarck, however, edited the telegram to make the ambassador's language appear more confrontational, and published it in newspapers in Berlin. Soon after, France was at war with Prussia and other states in the North German Confederation. The so-called Ems telegram was seen by many as a significant cause of aggression between France and Prussia, and importantly it made France out to be the aggressor.

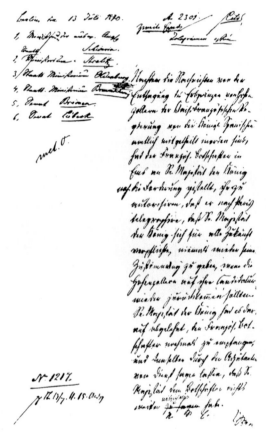

Figure 4.7 The editing and publishing of the Ems telegram was a skilful act on Bismarck's part. Not only did it spark war with France but it also made the French appear to be the aggressors

These events played a major role in German unification, as they made it appear that Germany as a whole was under attack. Bismarck put forth an impassioned plea to the southern German states, previously not members of the North German Confederation, in which he urged them to join Prussia in the fight against France. When all states agreed to join, a surge of patriotism swept through Germany and it appeared the country was united in its anti-French fervour.

The war was a short one. The Prussian-led army, with the support of units from all German states, won decisive victories, quickly forcing France's Napoleon III to surrender. This victory provided Otto von Bismarck with the power to negotiate a united Germany in which Prussian dominance was assured.

Therefore, it seems fair to argue that Bismarck's diplomatic skill – first, in drawing the French into a war and, second, in managing a unified force in a decisive defeat – was a significant factor in the eventual German unification of 1871.

On the other hand...

Some argue that Bismarck was in fact unreliable, possessed only superficial intelligence and was not forward thinking at all but rather reactionary. The historian J. Steinberg states that King William I of Prussia must have been desperate to appoint such a man as chief minister in 1862. The historian M. Fulbrook argues that Bismarck was probably 'less of an arch-manipulator than a clever exploiter of situations as they arose'. This perhaps limits the argument that Bismarck was the architect of German unification.

Overall

It seems fair to say that Bismarck was a skilled political operator, whether or not he always had a long-term plan in mind. The skill with which he exploited complex diplomatic situations, while simultaneously managing to maintain political unity in Prussia, was not only impressive but a major cause of eventual German unification. Certainly from the 1860s onwards, German unification appeared far from inevitable, and it seems fair to argue that Bismarck's actions played at least some role in the eventual unification of Germany in 1871.

4.1.5 Role of other countries

Some historians argue the role played by other countries, such as Britain and Russia, which were willing to accept Prussian dominance in Germany, enabled unification to transpire in 1871.

Britain

Britain appears to have been willing to accept growing Prussian dominance in Germany. Prussia was a Protestant country and therefore British rulers were predisposed to welcome Prussian **hegemony** over the German states. Moreover, Britain had long been mistrustful of French power and its leaders were happy to step back and allow any state to keep France in check, as Prussia appeared to be doing.

This made it more likely that Germany could be united in 1871, as it ensured that Britain, a major power in foreign policy terms, would stay out of European politics. In the absence of British interference, Prussia was able to defeat the Danes, Austrians and French unhindered.

Russia

Russia's lack of involvement in German politics was likewise important in enabling German unification in 1871. Even though Prussian liberals were critical of **autocratic** Russia, they were less critical than were the governments of Britain and France. This became clear during the Polish revolt (which came to be known as the January Uprising) in 1863–64. Although Bismarck reneged on his promise to hand over rebel Poles to the Russian **Tsar**, the Russian government was much more angry over British and French criticism. Moreover, Austria's handling of the Crimean War in 1853–56 enraged Russia, creating a situation where Russia was willing to accept Prussian gains in Austria.

This is important when considering the unification of Germany in 1871 as it meant that Russia was willing to see Prussian power grow at the expense of Austrian power. Despite the potential for conflict over the Polish revolt, Bismarck did enough to ensure that Prussia remained on friendly terms with Russia, leaving Prussia free to advance the cause of German unification.

On the other hand...

Although Britain and Russia were willing to accept growing Prussian power, neither country was active in supporting the state. They neglected to provide Prussia with military or financial aid and did not side with Bismarck in key conflicts. This suggests that other countries didn't play quite as important a role in the unification of Germany in 1871 as would first appear.

Overall

British and Russian neutrality during key periods of conflict did contribute to Prussia's ability to unify Germany under its leadership. In addition, Prussian diplomacy was successful in alienating Denmark, Austria and France, and this allowed the Prussian and later Prussian-led German army to defeat its opponents one at a time. Had major European powers been more active in checking Prussian power, then German unification would have been significantly harder to achieve. Indeed, Britain appears to have been quite willing to accept a powerful Prussia as a barrier to both rising French and Russian power.

Why was German unification achieved in 1871?

It is clear that multiple factors contributed to the unification of Germany in 1871, and the discussion in this chapter should help you to evaluate these factors. Prussia was an increasingly powerful actor in European politics, and growing military and economic might enabled Prussia to overcome neighbouring states and advance the cause of a united Germany under its leadership. Bismarck's political and diplomatic skill, be it based on long-term planning or short-term opportunism, created a situation in which unification could be achieved. Finally, the inaction of Britain and Russia during this period guaranteed there would be no powerful external state to prevent Germany from uniting.

ACTIVITIES

1 Create a mind map detailing all of the military and economic strengths possessed by Prussia. Aim to add at least eight different strengths to the map.

2 Explain how strong Prussian military leadership contributed to Prussian military victories in Europe against the Danes, Austrians and/or French.

3 Find three pieces of evidence to support the argument that Bismarck was a diplomatic expert.

4 Prioritise the importance of each factor, from most important to least important, in achieving the unification of Germany in 1871. Justify your most and least important factors.

5 Create an argument about what the most important reason for the unification of Germany was.
   a) Set out the argument in one sentence. What is the most important factor and why?
   b) Select three to four pieces of evidence to support this argument.
   c) Write three to four sentences of analysis to explain how this evidence supports the argument.
   d) Write three to four sentences to explain why this factor was more important than any other factor.

GLOSSARY

Term	Meaning
autocratic	Relating to a ruler who has absolute power.
Bundestag	The parliament of the German Confederation, which came into existence as a result of the Congress of Vienna in 1815.
dissolved	The official term for the end of a parliament.
hegemony	Leadership or dominance.
Junker	A Prussian noble or aristocrat.
Landwehr	A part-time militia that made up reserve forces in the German army.
Mobilisation (of troops)	The act of readying soldiers for military action.
realpolitik	A system of politics based on practical rather than moral or ideological considerations.
real terms	Referring to something's true value.
Tsar	A title used to designate the Russian emperor. Derived from the Latin word *caesar*, meaning 'emperor'.
ultimatum	A final demand or statement of terms.
Zollverein	A customs union of German states formed to manage tariffs and economic policies. It was created by the 1833 Zollverein treaties and formally started on 1 January 1834.

Chapter 5

An evaluation of the reasons why the Nazis achieved power in 1933

The aim of this chapter is to evaluate the reasons why the Nazis were able to come to power in Germany in 1933.

LINK TO EXAM

Higher

Key issue 5: this chapter will allow pupils to weigh up the relative importance of the reasons that contributed to the rise of the Nazis. This will allow pupils to judge the main factor or factors that led to the rise of Hitler and the Nazis.

Background

The First World War raged for four years, and all countries that fought endured terrible damage and loss. By late 1918 it was becoming increasingly clear that Germany was going to lose. The early stalemate of the first part of the war was, by 1918, a distant memory. New technology and tactics had created the war of movement that the generals had hoped for in 1914. In the final year of battle, momentum had tipped in the Allies' favour, and the entry of the USA would help to secure Allied victory on the Western Front.

Seeing the balance of power shifting, the Germans launched an offensive on the Western Front in the spring of 1918. Although successful in breaking through the British and French lines, the exhausted German troops soon ran out of munitions and supplies. The beleaguered troops were then faced with a massive Allied counterattack that successfully pushed the German troops out of France and Belgium, and back to the borders of Germany.

As the situation became increasingly dire in Germany, **Kaiser** Wilhelm II reluctantly accepted the need to introduce a degree of democracy to Germany under the leadership of Prince Maximilian von Baden. The army and aristocracy viewed this nascent democratic structure with total contempt, yet when the German naval commanders ordered a doomed naval engagement against the **blockading** British Royal Navy, the Kaiser lost control. Soldiers and sailors refused to follow orders, and instead set up Russian style 'soviets', or councils. Accepting the inevitable, Wilhelm II **abdicated**, Prince Maximilian von Baden resigned and Germany was declared a **republic**.

The first action of this new, provisional government was to sue for peace. In November 1918 an armistice was signed, democratic elections were held in January 1919 and a peace treaty was concluded in June at Versailles. The new German democratic government was dubbed the 'Weimar Republic'. Berlin was considered too dangerous a location for a government to sit, so instead the Thuringian city of Weimar was selected.

This new government was immediately beset by challenges. Disliked by those on the left as well as those on the right, the government was forced to face early challenges to its existence. Yet, it managed to weather the storm and by 1924 was entering a so-called 'Golden Age'.

However, by 1929 this stabilising period appeared to be a distant memory. The Wall Street Crash and ensuing global financial depression affected Germany badly. Financial crises, unpopular political decisions and a rise of political extremism all challenged the Weimar government.

During this period Weimar faced its greatest challenge from, among other parties, the increasingly powerful National Socialist German Workers' Party (NSDAP). The so-called 'Nazis' were led by Austrian-born German politician Adolf Hitler, and he and his party made vociferous calls for an immediate end to German democracy, blaming Germany's woes on Jewish people, **Bolsheviks** and German traitors.

By late 1932 the Nazis had gained sufficient political support to challenge the German president into allowing them to form a government. Foolishly, several established right-wing politicians believed that Hitler and the Nazi Party were little more than a disorganised mob which could be easily manipulated from behind the scenes. This turned out to be an error, and by January 1933 Hitler was officially recognised as the new chancellor of Germany.

In this chapter we will examine the reasons behind why Hitler and the Nazi Party were able to achieve such political power by 1933.

5.1 Why did the Nazis gain power in 1933?

For the purposes of the examination, it is important to be able to evaluate the reasons that led to the Nazis achieving power in 1933. This chapter sets out the key events and allows you to come to a conclusion about what the main factor or factors were that ultimately led to Nazi rule.

This section will examine the following factors:

Weaknesses of the Weimar Republic
Resentment towards the Treaty of Versailles
Economic difficulties
Appeal of Hitler and the Nazis after 1928
Weaknesses and mistakes of opponents

Understanding these issues will allow you to make a judgement on the main reason or reasons why the Nazi Party achieved power in 1933.

5.1.1 Weaknesses of the Weimar Republic

The elections that took place in January 1919 were the first free and democratic elections to take place in Germany since the fall of the monarchy. Soon after, in February, a parliament was set up. Friedrich Ebert, a member of the Social Democratic Party of Germany (SDP) was elected to the office of president, and centrist, pro-democracy parties won a significant majority. Approximately 82 per cent of eligible Germans voted in the election, around 75 per cent of whom cast their votes for either the SDP, the Centre Party (Zentrum, or Z for short) or the German Democratic Party (DDP).

Political spectrum	Radical left	Left	Moderate left	Centre	Moderate right	Right	Radical right
Common party name	Communists	Social Democrats	Democrats	Centre Party	People's Party	Nationalists	Nazis
Technical party name	KPD	SPD	DDP	Z	DNVP		NSDAP
	Independent Socialists						
	USPD						

Figure 5.1 The main political parties of the Weimar Republic

The first order of business for parliament was to draw up a new constitution. This established a **federal** German Republic governed by a president, parliament (**Reichstag**) and senate (**Reichsrat**). There were 17 federal regions (*Bundesländer*) and all Germans over the age of 20 could vote for representatives in a system of **proportional representation**. This constitution was approved by a vote of 262 to 75 in July 1919, with only nationalists and the Independent Social Democratic Party of Germany (USPD) opposing it. Otherwise, the system was lauded as being highly democratic. The contemporary historian G. Scheele even called it 'mechanically perfect'.

Yet, there is an argument that the Weimar Republic, even though it was in many ways a well-functioning democratic system, had fundamental weaknesses, which were exploited by Hitler and the Nazi Party, allowing them to take power in 1933.

Unpopularity

An underlying challenge facing Weimar was that some Germans were against democracy and the idea of a republican government.

One significant group which was deeply mistrustful of this new political system was the army. Though it was forced to be reduced in size after the end of the First World War and the passing of the Treaty of Versailles, the core of the old German army remained in post. Given the politically unstable times of the early Weimar Republic (more on this later), the government relied on the army to maintain law and order. However, as the historian R. Evans points out, the German officer corps remained 'fiercely monarchist and ultra-conservative'.

The same was true of the all-powerful civil service, which by the end of the 1920s was by far the biggest employer in Germany with over 700,000 people in post before 1923. The overwhelming majority of civil servants had been appointed in **autocratic** Germany, under the direction of the Kaiser and his ministers, and many struggled or were unwilling to adapt to the day-to-day business of democratic politics.

This was a significant weakness of the Weimar Republic. It meant that a majority of those the Weimar government relied upon to protect and advance the republic's agenda after the turmoil of 1918 had, in the words of R. Evans, 'little genuine loyalty to the constitution'. This weakened the Weimar Republic, making it more vulnerable to attacks from extremist parties such as the Nazis.

Moreover, many Weimar politicians were hugely unpopular due to the 'stab-in-the-back myth'. When the Treaty of Versailles was signed in 1919, it officially ended the First World War. Although it dictated arguably tough conditions for Germany, most historians agree the German government had little choice but to go along with the terms and sign it. However, regardless of the military or political reality, Field Marshal Hindenburg declared it 'shameful' that Ebert and other key Weimar politicians had accepted such terms. The politicians were labelled as 'unpatriotic' and 'November criminals'. Hindenburg even stated erroneously that the men responsible for 'stabbing the German army in the back' could have kept on fighting.

Figure 5.2 Field Marshal (later President) Hindenburg, who led the Imperial Germany Army during the First World War, was a vocal critic of the Weimar Republic

This had a major destabilising impact on the Weimar Republic. It encouraged extreme levels of political violence, endangering the lives of pro-Weimar politicians. Between 1919 and 1922 there were 376 political assassinations, 354 of which were carried out by right-wing terrorists. The treatment of those responsible for these murders highlighted the importance of the aforementioned 'old guard', as only 28 of the 354 assassins were sentenced. None received the death penalty, in stark contrast to the harsh punishments meted out to perpetrators of left-wing violence. This demonstrates the lack of support for the Weimar Republic among conservatives and nationalists, which weakened it, making it less able to resist attacks from extremists such as Hitler and the Nazi Party.

Unrest of the 1920s

There is also an argument that the Weimar government's political weaknesses during the 1920s highlighted its vulnerability, which enabled Hitler and the Nazis to achieve power in 1933.

One problem was the proportional representation (PR) election system. In this system, if a party achieved 15 per cent of the popular vote, it was awarded 15 per cent of the seats, and so on. By the 1920s there were around 30 political parties standing in Germany, resulting in a major fragmentation of the vote. This meant that it was very difficult for a single party to gain a majority and governments were likely to be coalitions of three or more parties. The process of forming coalitions was further hampered because parties such as the Communist Party of Germany (KPD) and the German National People's Party (DNVP) refused to join, instead calling for an end to the Weimar Republic. This led to unstable coalition government which shifted frequently. For example, in the years 1919 to 1930 there were 16 different coalition governments in Germany, each varying in nature and comprising different combinations of the centrist parties.

This was a huge drain on the Weimar Republic, as it made it harder to govern effectively. The frequent changing of ministers and governments arguably hampered Weimar's ability to fix the pressing social and economic challenges of the 1920s and 1930s. Of the seven governments formed between 1924 and 1930 only two were a majority, and the longest sitting government was in power for less than two years. This inability to sustain political continuity during a time of crisis damaged the republic's image, so much so that it made it possible for Hitler and the Nazi Party to undermine Weimar sufficiently to achieve power in 1933.

On the other hand…

It is perhaps wrong to argue that the Weimar government was doomed to fail. Several elements of the democratic system in Germany can be considered strengths, limiting the argument that it was a weak Weimar that led to Hitler and the Nazi Party's ascendancy to power.

First, although it is true the Weimar government was a series of coalitions, Germans were used to this form of politics. Coalitions were a deep-rooted part of German politics, as the pre-war system also led to coalitions, even though it used a different election system. This suggests that Germans were used to, or even expected, coalition government.

Additionally, although the PR system allowed for the representation of extremist parties such as the NSDAP and KPD, these parties remained in the minority in most Weimar elections. For example, in 1928, 76 per cent of voters supported pro-Weimar political parties, and the SPD led the 'Grand Coalition' of 1928, which held a comfortable majority in the Reichstag.

Moreover, as the socioeconomic and political situation stabilised in Germany between 1924 and 1929, there was a marked decline in political extremism. During this time there were no attempts to overthrow the government, fewer **paramilitary** groups were in operation and extremist representation in the Reichstag fell dramatically. For example, in the 1928 election the Nazi Party won just 2.6 per cent of the vote.

Finally, the constant changes to government have been somewhat overstated. While the official classification of Weimar governments altered, often the personnel did not. For example, Gustav Stresemann acted as foreign minister in nine consecutive governments and remained in office for more than six years. Heinrich Brauns remained as minister of labour in 12 governments between 1920 and 1928. This limits the argument that frequent elections precluded consistent policy implementation.

Overall

Nevertheless, it is clear that the structure of the Weimar Republic, as well as the views of those who staffed its important offices, arguably weakened Weimar. Some historians have argued that it became increasingly unclear who held ultimate authority under the Weimar constitution – the Reichstag or the president? – while frequent elections and the large number of parties became a source of derision for the Nazis.

The historian R. J. Evans examines these challenges faced by Weimar in more detail (Source 1).

Therefore, it seems fair to argue that, to one degree or another, the weaknesses of Weimar contributed to Hitler's ability to achieve power in 1933.

5.1.2 Resentment towards the Treaty of Versailles

In 1919, the leaders of the victorious Allied powers (Britain, France, Italy and the USA) met at the Palace of Versailles to discuss terms of surrender for Germany and its allies. Some Germans were quietly optimistic about the potential terms for a peace agreement. The Kaiser, whom many blamed for contributing to the outbreak of war, had fled Germany and was in exile. Germany had replaced its military autocracy with a democratic republic and expected to be able to enjoy self-determination as set out by the US president. However, the terms of the treaty were far harsher than many expected.

Table 5.1 Treaty of Versailles, summary of terms

Area	Summary of treaty terms
Territorial losses (Europe)	Losses without **plebiscite**: ● Alsace-Lorraine to France ● Eupen and Malmedy to Belgium ● Posen and West Prussia to Poland ● Memel to Lithuania ● City of Danzig became a free city Losses following a plebiscite: ● North Schleswig to Denmark The Rhineland region was demilitarised. The Saar region was placed under League of Nations control and administered by the French.
Military	Army restricted to 100,000 soldiers No conscription No tanks or heavy artillery Limited to 6 battleships, 6 cruisers and 12 destroyers Remaining naval vessels to be surrendered to the British
Colonies	All colonies lost, to become League of Nations **mandates**
Reparations	Article 231 of the treaty held Germany responsible for starting the war and therefore liable to pay for all damage. Germany's initial level of reparation was £6600 million (132 billion marks).

While there remains much debate as to whether or not the peace treaty was too harsh, this section of the chapter primarily examines how the treaty was received by the German people. This will allow you to evaluate whether or not resentment towards the Treaty of Versailles was a significant factor behind Hitler and the Nazi Party's rise to power in 1933.

The treaty as a *diktat*

The Treaty of Versailles was viewed by many Germans as being unfair, as it imposed unreasonably harsh conditions on Germany.

First, German negotiators were excluded from treaty discussions until the last stage of the negotiation process. This meant the Allies determined among themselves what punishments Germany should be faced with, and then the terms were delivered to the German government through a *diktat*, which the government had little choice but to accept. Perhaps the harshest of these terms was that Germany was to take sole blame for causing the war, and therefore would be responsible for the financial reconstruction of the lands it occupied via a system of financial reparations.

Whether or not these terms were proportionate with the benefit of hindsight is perhaps immaterial to our question. What is certain is that this 'dictated peace' caused a great deal of resentment throughout Germany. The terms were deemed to be unreasonably harsh, particularly given that those Germans responsible for war had now been removed from power. Indeed, the leaders of the Weimar Republic even asked Hindenburg for an assessment about the German army's ability to resist should they refuse to accept the terms of the treaty and the war be restarted.

However, in reality the government had little choice but to accept the Allies' terms, leading the outrage many Germans felt to be targeted at the centrist politicians of the Weimar Republic. Given that the army denied any military failure on its part, it became easy to blame the leaders of the Weimar Republic for surrendering unnecessarily. They became known as the 'November criminals' because they had 'stabbed Germany in the back'. Hitler and the Nazis would go on to exploit this lack of popularity, which helped them to achieve power in 1933.

Count Brockdorff-Rantzau, a diplomat and the main German envoy in attendance at Versailles, commented on the draft terms of the treaty on 7 May 1919 (Source 2).

SOURCE 2

We are required to admit that we alone are war-guilty; such an admission from my lips would be a lie. We are far from seeking to exonerate Germany from all responsibility for the fact that this world war broke out and was waged as it was. The attitude of the former German Government at The Hague Peace Conferences, their actions and omissions in the tragic twelve days of July, may have contributed to the calamity, but we emphatically combat the idea that Germany, whose people were convinced that they were waging a defensive war, bears the sole guilt.

Transcript adapted from the National Archives website: https://www.nationalarchives.gov. uk/education/greatwar/transcript/g5cs1s3t.htm

The financial reparations that this guilt conveyed were likewise deemed to be too harsh by many contemporaries. Even some key British commentators viewed them as severe, with the British economist John Maynard Keynes arguing that they would 'reduce Germany to servitude for a generation'. Reparation payments ran into hundreds of billions of marks, and some argued that they were too high to ever be repayable. It was assumed by many that this was an intentional move, to crush the German economy and render it incapable of recovery.

Again, whether the level of repayment was fair or not, the high level of reparations demanded by the Allies was met with great resentment in Germany. Many Germans felt they were being exploited as unfortunate losers of a war not of their own making. For example, the right-wing press fiercely opposed the idea of transferring money and resources to rebuild the economies of the victorious countries. Hitler was able to exploit this sense of national outrage in his quest for power.

Land clauses

The treaty also forced Germany to cede much productive and valuable land to the Allies. Again, while many of these conditions were arguably proportionate, such as the return of Alsace-Lorraine to France after the Germans annexed it in their victory over France in 1871, they were greeted with hostility and resentment in Germany.

Germany was forced to transfer several other large areas of territory to neighbouring states, including Memel to Lithuania, Eupen and Malmedy to Belgium, West Prussia, Posen and Upper Silesia to Poland and North Schleswig to Denmark. In addition, all colonies were lost.

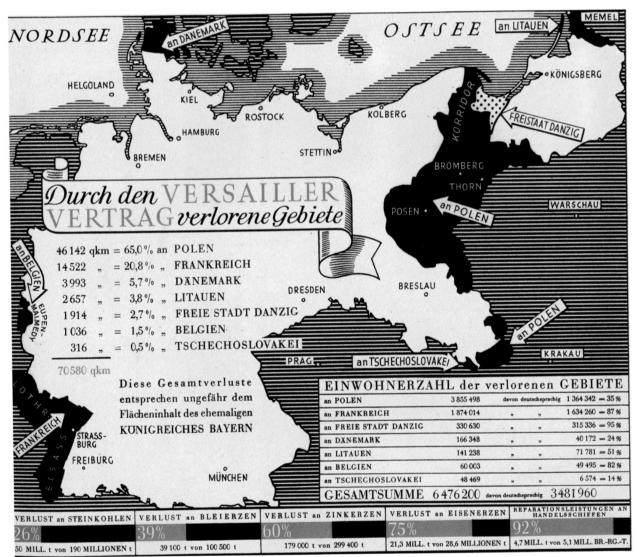

Figure 5.3 The Treaty of Versailles required Germany to give up large tracts of land as punishment for starting the war, which resulted in 6 million Germans being forced to live as citizens of other states. This was seen as a huge humiliation by many in Germany, especially nationalists and those on the right

This loss of territory caused outrage in Germany, as it seemed to many that the Germans were being unfairly targeted on the principle of national determination. Not only was Germany forced into giving up so much land – the only First World War power to face such losses – but also 6 million Germans were now living outside the Weimar Republic. This was seen as a humiliating and unfair punishment, one that would later be exploited by Hitler when he called for an end to the treaty terms and the return of these lands to Germany.

On the other hand...

There is an argument to suggest that although the terms of the treaty were initially a shock to many Germans, as time passed the blow softened. The most challenging time for Weimar appeared to be between 1919 and 1923, when the government was faced with the initial outrage and economic impact of the treaty terms. Yet, Weimar was able to weather the storm, negotiate financial assistance from the USA under the 1924 Dawes Plan, and build political stability into the late 1920s. This suggests that the Treaty of Versailles may not have been the main reason behind Hitler becoming chancellor in January 1933.

Overall

However, it is important to note the shock with which the Treaty of Versailles was received. This is highlighted by the historian S. Lee (Source 3).

SOURCE 3

Versailles created a deep and widespread resentment throughout the entire population. Germans had already suffered severely during the closing stages of the war as a direct result of the British blockade, and they assumed that Germany would have a genuine share of any post-war settlement. Hence, although they expected [some loss of territory] the actual terms came as a profound blow.

Lee, S. (2010) *The Weimar Republic* (2nd edn), Routledge

The events of the Kapp Putsch (1920) offer particularly compelling supporting evidence that the Versailles terms were outright unacceptable to many. Following the government's plan to demilitarise, thereby adhering to the treaty terms, the right-wing politician Dr Wolfgang Kapp attempted to overthrow the Weimar government in protest. The German army, bitterly angry at the government's proposed demilitarisation, refused to provide protection and crush the revolt. The right-wing threat to the government only failed thanks to a combination of a **general strike**, the lack of active support from within the military and the refusal of most civil servants to follow Kapp's orders.

Overall, given that the treaty would come to be connected, fairly or unfairly, to future economic hardship, and that many Germans believed Weimar politicians to have betrayed Germany, we can say that resentment towards Versailles played at least some role in the Nazi Party's rise to power in 1933.

5.1.3 Economic difficulties

Many historians have connected the economic troubles of the Weimar Republic to the rise of the Nazis. This is perhaps best exemplified by the historian A. J. P. Taylor's argument that Hitler's rise was a result of the Great Depression. This section will evaluate the importance of the argument that Hitler's rise was possible thanks to Weimar's economic difficulties.

1918–23

The German economy was severely impacted by Germany's defeat in the First World War. The war had seen a dramatic rise in Germany's debt, which between 1913 and 1919 had grown from 5000 million to 144,000 million marks. This was magnified by high levels of inflation that could only be controlled by increasing tax or cutting government spending, neither popular policies in post-war European politics.

The dire economic situation was exacerbated by the impact of the British wartime naval blockade. Just as the German navy had attempted to force Britain out of the war through unrestricted submarine warfare, Britain had likewise tried to starve Germany out of the war through imposing the blockade. Such was the impact of this policy, in 1918 alone 293,000 Germans died from starvation and pneumonia. The blockade also crippled German trade, and reduced imports and exports to nearly nil.

The effects were made worse by the financial burden of reparations. By 1921 Germany was expected to repay 2.5 billion marks a year. Unable to keep up repayments, the Weimar Republic had to print money to keep the economy running and began defaulting on its payments. The French, believing that Germany could afford to pay its debts but was refusing to do so, sent troops to invade the Ruhr, Germany's main industrial region, in an attempt to secure their reparation payments through the confiscation of industrial goods. This action was justified under the terms of the Treaty of Versailles.

In response, Weimar ordered coal mine, factory, rail and steel workers to strike and refuse assistance to foreign troops under a policy known as 'passive resistance'. The government continued to pay the striking workers' wages by ramping up the printing of money, contributing to rising hyperinflation and leading to economic collapse.

Figure 5.4 Employers take the money needed to pay workers for the week. Photos such as this show how extreme hyperinflation had become, with paper money now more or less worthless. Although hyperinflation would be effectively eliminated in 1923 by Stresemann and other Weimar politicians, some Germans continued to blame the Weimar government for allowing it to happen in the first place

The economic impact of the Ruhr Crisis of 1923 was huge. The government decision to print banknotes to float the economy accelerated hyperinflation, and by the end of 1923 the foreign exchange rate was 4.2 trillion marks to 1 US dollar. Nearly 200 factories were employed to print money, and the price of food skyrocketed. Germans with savings, or whose wages failed to keep pace with this rampant inflation, suffered greatly. This weakened the Weimar Republic, as it appeared that a democratic government could not deliver a stable economy. Weimar politicians were attacked as self-serving, or willing to see middle- and working-class Germans suffer while the elite took advantage of inflation to pay off their debts and mortgages with worthless money. Right-wing anti-Republican sentiment was also on the rise, challenging the Weimar government and making its rule less stable. This atmosphere of discontent enabled Hitler to bring his own challenge to Weimar.

1924–28

However, after the Ruhr crisis, Germany was able to enter a short period of relative stability and growth, which has since been dubbed Weimar's 'Golden Age'. This economic recovery was based on the introduction of a new currency underpinned by US loans in a scheme called the Dawes Plan. However, there remained signs that the German economic recovery may not have been complete.

For one, unemployment remained constant in Germany during this period, with levels never falling below 1.3 million. This was approaching a pre-Depression high of nearly 3 million by 1929.

There were also problems with the German import/export balance. The Weimar government had striven to protect workers' rights and social justice through expensive schemes like social insurance. This meant that German goods were more expensive to produce, negatively impacting exports. Moreover, Weimar policies appeared to neglect farmers and agricultural workers, instead focusing on the development of cities.

This may have contributed to the rise of the Nazi Party, as it is perhaps fair to argue that while German economic recovery seemed strong on the surface during the Golden Age, the foundations remained weak. The government was running the economy based on huge loans and with a poor import/export balance, meaning the German economy was particularly vulnerable to changes in the global market. This also led seemingly to the neglect of certain groups in society, such as farmers, leading those who felt they were missing out in the new economy to turn to the promise of more extreme politicians.

1929–33

The German economy collapsed spectacularly in the late 1920s and early 1930s, a period that coincided with a dramatic increase in support for the Nazis. This has led some historians to claim that economic collapse was the biggest factor in Hitler achieving power in 1933.

In 1929, the US stock market crashed. The value of stocks plummeted and desperate investors tried to limit their losses by selling their entire portfolios. This ruined the lives of millions of Americans and compelled the US government to call in foreign loans to aid economic recovery. However, given that German economic recovery had relied on these loans, this caused extreme financial damage to the German economy. The impact was felt nearly immediately. Industrial production fell by around 40 per cent, around 50,000 businesses went bankrupt, wages fell in real terms and unemployment soared. By late 1932 there were nearly 6 million unemployed Germans.

The economic crash further discredited the Weimar government, which was once again blamed for financial instability. Many working Germans felt financially insecure, or they relied on low-paid or casual work to survive. Farmers were equally badly hit, and the events deepened the agricultural depression already under way in rural regions. Moreover, homelessness, poverty and destitution all increased. Under the pressures of extreme economic hardship, many Germans became more likely to turn to extreme politics for answers.

The German system of social security was unable to cope with such acute pressures, and political squabbles soon emerged. The crash caused a schism in the 1928 'Grand Coalition', causing the SPD chancellor Hermann Müller (1928–30) to resign due to refusing to tackle unemployment. President Hindenburg dissolved the Reichstag when it failed to approve a budget. Centre Party leader Heinrich Brüning was appointed chancellor, yet he lacked a majority in the Reichstag and so relied on a series of emergency decrees to pass laws.

This period highlighted the economic difficulties that Weimar faced, and there is a clear connection between this instability and the rise in extremist support. In the 1930 Reichstag elections the KPD won 77 seats and the NSDAP 107. This made it impossible to form a moderate coalition. Moreover, given that Brüning was able to pass only 29 minor bills during his time as chancellor (March 1930–May 1932) but enacted no fewer than 109 emergency decrees, it suggests he was ruling more as a semi-dictator. Finally, his policies of cutting unemployment benefits and increasing taxes may have helped balance the budget but they were extremely unpopular. They even earned him the nickname 'the Hunger Chancellor'. Taken together, this generated a great deal of resentment towards the Weimar Republic and pushed many Germans to extreme politics.

Figure 5.5 Germans searching for pieces of coal among the mud so they could heat their homes and avoid common diseases like pneumonia. Scenes like this were all too common across the country during the economic hardship of the 1930s

On the other hand…

It would be wrong to suggest that the Weimar Republic faced constant economic hardship. The hyperinflation of 1923 was quickly and effectively tackled by the Weimar government, and it did so without raising taxes or cutting benefits. Moreover, the extreme inflation in the run-up to 1923 allowed for rapid economic growth and high levels of employment. This has led to some experts calling the inflation of 1919–22 'good' inflation.

Additionally, during the Golden Age of 1924–29 the Weimar Republic demonstrated economic progress. German workers enjoyed increased protection and social security, exports rose by almost 40 per cent and there was a high degree of foreign investment.

Perhaps, then, economic difficulties were not the main reason why Hitler was able to become chancellor in 1933.

Overall

That being said, it is clear that the Weimar government's inability to fix the crumbling German economy, and seemingly making it worse through Brüning's policy of austerity, aided the growth of extremism in Germany. The historian H. Mommsen argues that Brüning was 'preparing the ground for Hitler and the conservative right' – in other words, the economic fallout of the Great Depression had a huge political impact on the Weimar Republic. Clearly, many Germans turned to extreme political parties in search of resolution, as evidenced in the election results of this period. For example, in 1928, pre-Crash, the Nazis won only 2.6 per cent of the vote. By 1930 this had increased to 18.3 per cent, and at the end of 1932, when unemployment was at its peak, the Nazi Party won 33.1 per cent of the vote. Clearly, then, we can argue that there is at least some correlation between the economic difficulties of Weimar and Hitler and the Nazi Party's rise to power.

5.1.4 Appeal of Hitler and the Nazis after 1928

The Nazi Party (NSDAP, or Nazis) had reformed under Adolf Hitler's leadership in 1921. It followed an extreme-right agenda, including ultra-nationalism, racism, authoritarianism and anti-capitalism. Hitler slowly became an increasingly well-known political figure, reaching the national stage after his failed attempt to take over the Bavarian and the national government in 1923. Some historians argue that it was he and his party's ideas after 1928 that led to their rise to power by 1933.

Nazi ideas and propaganda

Nazi policies were not a coherent agenda, more a collection of semi-connected ideas designed to appeal to every class within society. Many Germans felt they could identify with at least some of these policies.

For example, Nazi policies called for the return of 'German land' to Germany. Given that by 1928, 6 million Germans were living outside the borders of Weimar Germany, this idea appealed to many nationalists.

Hitler also promised to ignore the Treaty of Versailles and rearm the military. He declared that this would allow Germany to claim rightful *lebensraum*, or living space, in the East. This was combined with the idea of German racial superiority, which was based on the claim that as a 'Nordic' people, Germans were 'superior' to ethnic groups of Slavic, Jewish and southern European people. Hitler provided the convenient scapegoat of the Jewish people as a reason for all of Germany's woes. Moreover, the Nazis were staunchly anti-communist, and emphasised family values and traditions.

This cocktail of ideas appealed to citizens across Germany. It gave them both someone to blame (Jewish people) for all of Germany's troubles, and apparent hope for the future. This future included a return of German land, a restoration of German pride and territorial expansion eastwards, providing further wealth. While these policies were not explained fully, nor did they contain any practical details, they appealed to many of those hit hard by the period of economic hardship. Moreover, Hitler's anti-communist stance won him support from powerful businessmen and financiers, lending the Nazis credibility and crucial funds. This contributed to the Nazi election breakthrough in the early 1930s, which was fundamental to their achieving power in 1933.

While the Nazi message was popular among many Germans, the way it was communicated was very effective too. The Nazi propaganda machine was steered by Joseph Goebbels, chief propagandist for the Nazi Party and, later, Reich Minister of Propaganda (1933–45). Goebbels ran all Nazi election campaigns, through which he established the Nazis as a *volkspartei*, or People's Party. This enabled the Nazis to claim they represented all Germans, rather than one class in particular. Nazi rallies were likewise well managed, exciting and popular. Moreover, strategic poster campaigns attacked opponents of Nazism as well as helping to develop the cult of Hitler.

Through Goebbels' propaganda machine and his ability to 'bend' the party's message to suit the audience, the Nazis were able to win popular support and secure votes, which set them on the path to eventual power in 1933.

Figure 5.6 Joseph Goebbels during the spring election campaign of 1932. Goebbels was able to craft simple yet effective propaganda, which supported Hitler and the Nazi Party in their quest for power

The role of Hitler

Without Hitler as their political leader, it could be argued that the Nazi Party might not have achieved power in 1933. Through his sheer force of personality he was able to maintain unification of the far-right, and place his brutal stamp on the party.

Hitler was an especially impressive orator, and he used this to great effect in dramatic political speeches, which energised his base and won him legions of supporters.

The historian J. Caplan comments on Hitler's abilities as a speaker (Source 4).

This suggests that Hitler's leadership played an important role in his achieving power by 1933. His speeches succeeded in solidifying his support, uniting the party, its members and supporters under his banner, and generating excitement about his vision for a resurgent Germany.

On the other hand…

Much of Hitler's rhetoric focused on abandoning the Treaty of Versailles. This included the expansion of German military power and territory in the east, and bringing an end to reparations. Yet, by 1929 many of these issues had become less important to ordinary Germans, suggesting that Nazi policies may not fully explain Hitler's rise to power.

Overall

Clearly Nazi policies played at least some role in the party's rise to power. However, while many have argued that it was Hitler's anti-Versailles stance that led to the party gaining widespread support, perhaps of even greater importance was his unflinching stance towards communists. Given that communist support was also rising during the tough times of the early 1930s, many Germans turned to Hitler and the Nazis as the presumed best chance at preventing the infiltration of communist ideas into Germany from Bolshevik Russia. This helped to win support from all sectors in society, including farmers and agricultural workers, the middle class and wealthier Germans, which helps to explain why the Nazis achieved power by 1933.

5.1.5 Weaknesses and mistakes of opponents

It was not only the actions of Hitler and the Nazi Party, and the challenges and weaknesses of Weimar, which helped the Nazis achieve power by 1933, but also the weaknesses and mistakes of their opponents.

Disunity of the 'left'

A significant factor in enabling Hitler and the Nazis to achieve political power was perhaps disunity among the left. Had the political parties on the left been able to work together then the Nazis would have found it significantly harder to disrupt the political process in Germany. The main split on the left was between the Communist Party (KPD), Independent Socialists (USPD) and Social Democrats (SPD). One source of tension lay in the willingness of the SPD to use military force to suppress the KPD and USPD.

For example, the Spartacist Revolt was an attempt by militant **socialists** under the leadership of Karl Liebknecht and Rosa Luxemburg to overthrow the Weimar Republic in January 1919. The SPD-dominated Weimar government relied on paramilitary troops called the Freikorps to suppress the uprising. The Freikorps consisted of embittered ex-soldiers and nationalists, and they despised communists. They operated almost outside the law and used brutal violence to supress the revolt. Hundreds were killed or summarily executed, including Luxemburg and Liebknecht, in the so-called 'Battle for Berlin'. Encouraged by this success, the defence minister Gustav Noske, also a member of the SPD, ordered the Freikorps to suppress similar revolts in Bremen, Hamburg and the Ruhr.

Figure 5.7 Soldiers crew a machine gun from a Berlin tenement flat in 1919. The Spartacist uprising showed how willing the SPD-dominated Weimar government was to use brutal violence against others on the left. Some historians argue that this detracted from the Marxist doctrine which underpinned some of the SPD's policies

This played a significant role in weakening the left, leaving German politics more susceptible to right-wing action. Communists and independent socialists were shocked by the SPD's brutal response and were permanently unwilling to cooperate with the party politically. The hard-left's unwillingness to work with moderate socialists, and determination to redouble calls for the end of Weimar democracy, left centrist politics more vulnerable to attacks from right-wing extremists. Hitler and the Nazis pounced on events such as this, using them as evidence to demonstrate the chaos Germany was in, suggesting a strong leader was needed to maintain law and order. We can therefore argue that it was this disunity of the left that aided Hitler's rise to power.

Schemes of the 'right'

It was not just disunity of the left that aided Hitler's rise, but also mistakes made by elements of the political elite in Germany. This idea centres on the nature of the Weimar Constitution, in which the president was required to select the chancellor and invite them to form a government. Given the frequency with which governments were being overturned and reformed, this was an important presidential power.

The decision of how to form a government became particularly acute after Brüning's dismissal in May 1932. One of the main actors in the coming race for power was Kurt von Schleicher, a former general, nationalist, confidant of Hindenburg and a man with his own political aspirations. He viewed the Nazis as a tool with which to defeat the communists and secure his own power as chancellor. Schleicher envisaged a form of 'presidential government', in which the Reichstag would be sidelined and the old conservative elite could regain the power it had lost in 1918. Hoping to woo an increasingly popular Hitler, Schleicher took evasive action in mid-1932. He advised Hindenburg to install the far-right Franz von Papen as chancellor, lifted the ban on the Sturmabteilung (the SA), a key Nazi paramilitary group, illegally dismissed the anti-Nazi government of Prussia, and held an election to allow the Nazis to consolidate their political position.

The Nazis performed exceptionally well in the July 1932 federal election, becoming the largest party in the Reichstag (although they failed to win a majority). However, Hitler was loathe to play along with Schleicher's game and he refused to join any right-wing coalition unless he was named chancellor. President Hindenburg, still convinced that Hitler was not fit for such a post, refused his offer. Instead, Schleicher formed a government, but without the support of Hitler and the Nazi Party the government failed.

Another election was held in November 1932, the results of which saw a drop in Nazi support from the previous high. Hindenburg, fearing that a snubbed Hitler would disrupt any future government not led by the Nazis, invited him to become chancellor. Hitler accepted and was sworn in as chancellor of Germany in January 1933. Vice Chancellor Papen joked that he had 'hired' Hitler, and that the Nazis would be easy to control now that they were in government. However, history went on to prove him wrong.

Clearly the machinations of the German aristocratic elite played a major role in enabling Hitler to become chancellor. Their assessment that Hitler could be controlled was deeply misguided, and essentially led them to hand him the keys to power. It was they who panicked and thrust Hitler into the chancellery, therefore completing his rise to power in January 1933.

On the other hand…

It is worth noting that the only reason the German elite took such interest in Hitler was because he was the leader of the largest party in the Reichstag. Convention alone dictated that it should be he whom the president asked to form a government. This perhaps limits the argument that the scheming of the right was the most important factor in Hitler achieving power in 1933.

Additionally, although the communists may have felt betrayed by the social democrats, other Germans were probably relieved that the Nazi Party was willing to take a strong anti-communist stance. Therefore, although this action cost the SPD support from the left, it may have helped the SPD cooperate with future coalitions as the 1920s and 1930s progressed.

Overall

It is clear that there were many factors influencing Hitler's rise to power. The nature of the Weimar Republic and the economic and political challenges it faced are intertwined with the rise of the Nazis. So too is the political stance of the Nazis and the role of Hitler himself. These factors created an atmosphere in which the traditional elite in Germany were convinced that Hitler could be a useful tool to advance their own interests. Alas, this strategy backfired with profound impact.

ACTIVITIES

1 Select five or more pieces of evidence which support the argument that the Weimar Republic was too weak (in either its structure or policies) to endure in postwar Germany.

2 Select three counterarguments to the idea that Weimar was too weak to survive.

3 Make a case as to whether or not you believe that Weimar was doomed to fail.
   a) Did it have a chance to survive? Write an argument in one to two sentences.
   b) What evidence supports this argument? Select two to three pieces of evidence.

4 Summarise the impact that Hitler and the Nazi Party had on their journey to achieve power in 1933. Write three to five sentences.

5 Create a table or mind map that categorises all of the strengths and weaknesses of the Weimar Republic.

6 What evidence is there to suggest that the economic depression of the 1930s was the main reason why the Nazis were able to achieve power by 1933? Select three pieces of evidence.

GLOSSARY

Term	Meaning
abdication	When a monarch gives up the throne.
autocratic	Relating to a ruler who has absolute power.
blockade	An act or means of sealing off a place to prevent goods or people from entering or leaving.
Bolshevik	A member of the Russian revolutionary party of the Bolsheviks.
diktat	A harsh penalty or settlement imposed upon a defeated party by the victor.
federal	A system of government in which individual regions have a large number of powers but pool responsibility for economic and military policy.
general strike	When a group of industrial workers refuse to work en masse in an organised attempt to achieve economic or political objectives.
inflation	A general increase in prices and a fall in the purchasing value of money.
Kaiser	The German emperor.
mandate	The authority given to a government or person to act in a particular way, such as run a region or country, usually as a result of an election.
paramilitary	An organised, though unofficial, military force.
plebiscite	The direct vote of all the members of an electorate on an important public question, such as a change in the constitution.

proportional representation	A system through which political parties gain seats in proportion to the number of votes cast for them.
Reichsrat	A senate-style assembly in which each region had equal representation during the period of the Weimar Republic.
Reichstag	Germany's parliament during the period of the Weimar Republic and the Second Reich.
reparations	Compensation for war damage paid by a defeated state.
republic	A state in which supreme power is held by elected representatives.
socialist	A person who advocates socialism, a political, social and economic system characterised by public, rather than private, ownership.
soviet	A council of workers or soldiers that makes democratic decisions about how they should act.

Chapter 6

An evaluation of the reasons why the Nazis were able to stay in power, 1933–39

The aim of this chapter is to evaluate the reasons why the Nazis were able to stay in power between 1933 and 1939.

LINK TO EXAM

Higher

Key issue 6: this chapter will allow pupils to judge the relative importance of the factors that allowed Hitler and the Nazis to stay in power, 1933–39.

Background

For the reasons discussed in the previous chapter, Hitler was asked to become chancellor of Germany in January 1933, and to form a government. Though the president, Paul von Hindenburg, thought that Hitler was ultimately unsuitable to fill the post of chancellor, he was compelled to let the Nazis into government given the failures of consecutive coalitions during the 1930s. It seems Hindenburg was willing to accept the advice of close friends and advisers, who assured Hindenburg that Hitler could be easily controlled.

Yet, as mentioned at the close of Chapter 5, history proved these men wrong. Hitler not only established a Nazi government but went on to forge a seemingly immovable **fascist** regime. This regime appeared to operate from an increasingly secure position and introduced radical reforms to Germany. It sought to build a new society, a new economy and new political power. The policies advocated were extreme, exclusionist and murderous. Hitler and the Nazi Party are correctly identified as architects of genocide, racial hate and **totalitarianism**.

With the benefit of hindsight, it appears strange that Hitler was able to advance such views and remain so firmly in power during the 1930s. The question, then, is how was this possible? How was it that Hitler and the Nazis were able to control Germany so effectively during the years leading up to the Second World War?

The answer, perhaps, lies in a combination of factors. For one, it is clear that Hitler acted quickly to assert his control over German politics and daily life. This so-called **Gleichschaltung** was an effort by Hitler and the Nazis to make all local authorities subordinate to Nazi control. Hitler further strengthened his position in the wake of the Reichstag fire (27 February 1933) and the violent purge of the **Sturmabteilung** (30 June–2 July 1934). This element of fear was extended beyond internal threats to the population at large. The SS, Gestapo and concentration camps all seem to have played, to one degree or another, some role in co-opting many Germans to at least 'go along' with Hitler's rule.

Other Germans, conversely, may have been enticed by pervasive Nazi **propaganda** to support Nazi rule. Nazi techniques for controlling mass media, including the use of emerging technologies like the radio and cinema newsreels, may have played a role in convincing Germans that Nazi rule was beneficial. In addition, the economic policies set out by Hitler's finance minister Hjalmar Schacht (1934–37) appeared to 'fix' the broken Germany economy, helping it to recover after the impact of the Great Depression. Nazi policy focused not only on the cities – policies such as Blut und Boden ('Blood and Soil') appealed to many farmers, who had grown tired of the depreciation of the agricultural economy.

Others may have been swayed by the Nazi Party's social policies. Policies linked to women, youth groups, school curriculums, the composition of society and religion all played a role in helping Hitler to stay in power until 1939 and beyond.

The question, therefore, is what was the most significant factor enabling Hitler and the Nazi Party to maintain control of Germany between 1933 and 1939?

6.1 Why were the Nazis able to stay in power, 1933–39?

For the purposes of the examination, it is important to be able to evaluate the reasons that helped the Nazis stay in power between 1933 and 1939. This chapter sets out the main factors in why Hitler and the Nazi Party were able to retain power and supports you in evaluating their relative importance.

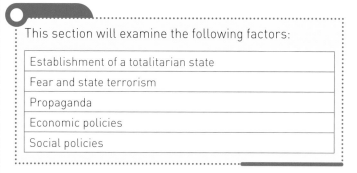

This section will examine the following factors:

Establishment of a totalitarian state
Fear and state terrorism
Propaganda
Economic policies
Social policies

Understanding these issues will allow you to form a judgement on what the main reason or reasons were for why the Nazis were able to stay in power.

6.1.1 Establishment of a totalitarian state

One reason why the Nazis were able to stay in power between 1933 and 1939 was because of the powerful political control the party exercised over the German state. Some historians argue that the legal control Hitler had over the day-to-day government of Germany enabled him to stay in power in the years leading up to the Second World War.

1933: the Reichstag fire and the Enabling Act

When Hitler became chancellor, his position was not fully secure. Though he was leader, he was expected to operate within the democratic framework of the Weimar Republic. This involved meetings, debates with coalition partners and the mundane day-to-day work of democratic politics. None of this interested Hitler, who was reported to be very lazy, but it also detracted from the **authoritarian** government he wanted to create. Therefore, the Nazis took several steps in 1933 to undermine democracy and create a system of government where they had almost total control.

The first of these came after the Reichstag fire. On 27 February 1933, the German parliament building, the Reichstag, was allegedly set alight by the Dutch communist council member Marinus van der Lubbe. Using this event as pretext to claim that communists were plotting against the government, Hitler passed the Decree of the Reich President for the Protection of the People and the State on 28 February. This effectively banned the Communist Party (KPD) in Germany and eroded many of the fundamental rights Germans had been given under the Weimar Constitution.

The Nazis then announced that they would hold an election in March 1933, through which they hoped to use the myth that Germany was under attack from the left to increase their support. Hitler used the context of the fire to frame the election as a last-ditch attempt to prevent the spread of communism in Germany, and the Nazis distributed large quantities of anti-communist propaganda. The results of the election were poorer than the Nazis hoped: they failed to secure an absolute majority for their party. However, the Nationalist Party (DNVP) agreed to cooperate with the Nazis, giving the Nazi Party a majority in the Reichstag.

Hitler used this majority to pass the Enabling Law on 23 March 1933, formally entitled the Law for the Removal of Distress from People and the **Reich**. This gave him the power to amend the Weimar Constitution without prior approval from the president or the **Reichsrat**. In effect, this allowed Hitler to rule as a dictator, passing decrees rather than debating democratic laws. The Enabling Act was used to ban trade unions in May and the Social Democrats (SPD) from June 1933. It also allowed the government to set up a new system of local administration in which Nazi governors (*Gauleiters*) ran the German states. It was also used to pass the Law for the Restoration of the Professional Civil Service on 7 April. This removed Jews and political opponents from the civil service, police and courts, and the school system. The law also affected university professors, who were all civil servants. Those dismissed included prominent scientists, who emigrated to the UK, the USA and elsewhere.

Both the events of the Reichstag fire and the passing of the Enabling Act allowed Hitler to maintain control of Germany as through them he was able to effectively attain the powers of a legal dictator. He had created a system in which he could use these legal powers to sideline his opponents. He was able not only to remove his political opponents from the political process, but also to establish a system where government employees were loyal to him and the Nazi Party through his purge of the civil service. Hitler was able to ensure the spread of this legal dictatorship across all regions of Germany by using the Gauleiters to enforce Nazi government in each of the German states. It was perhaps all these powers taken together that enabled Hitler to remain in control in Germany from 1933 to 1939.

1934: Hitler as the Führer

Despite the wide-ranging political powers granted by the Enabling Act, Hitler still was not completely secure in his position. While his political opponents had been sidelined, he was increasingly concerned about the rising power of the Sturmabteilung (SA). These brown-shirted Nazis had played a significant part in Hitler's rise but were growing in size and importance. The leader of the SA, Ernst Röhm, was critical of some of Hitler's policies, and wanted to merge the SA and the army to create a People's Army. Such an idea was abhorrent to the army, which disliked the ill-disciplined SA. Hitler became convinced that Röhm posed a serious threat to his power, and so an operation was launched to purge the upper ranks of the SA.

In the early hours of 30 June 1934, Operation Hummingbird (*Unternehmen Kolibri*) was launched. Dubbed 'The Night of the Long Knives', it saw **Schutzstaffel (SS)** units mount a series of attacks on SA leaders across Germany. At least 200 people were killed, including SA commanders like Röhm. Old opponents, including Schleicher, were also killed.

Figure 6.1 The SA was becoming too large and influential within the Nazi Party, and Hitler feared Rohm (centre) would try to replace him as leader. This alone was motivation enough to encourage Hitler to purge the SA, with the help of the SS and the army

These events helped Hitler to stay in power as he was able to remove any potential opposition from within his own party. The ruthlessness with which he did this also enabled him to stamp his total dominance on the party. Moreover, by taking action against the unpopular SA, Hitler had improved his standing in the eyes of the army and the president, both of which helped him consolidate his position as chancellor.

On the other hand…

While it appeared that Hitler was able to assert total control over Germany by 1934, this may not have been entirely correct. There remained several regions that were reluctant to work with Nazi officials. For example, in some areas of rural Bavaria local men volunteered to be Nazi administrators not because they wanted to consolidate Hitler's power but rather because they hoped to mitigate the influence of rural decrees and to maintain established traditions, such as religious festivals. This suggests that Hitler's control may not have been total, therefore limiting the argument that this was the main factor for his retaining power between 1933 and 1939.

Overall

That being said, it is clear that Hitler had established a strong political position as early as 1934. He had used the democratic system to build a one-party state with himself as dictator. He had removed opponents within and outside the Nazi Party and struck a deal with the army. This helped to secure his position and built the foundations for his eventual control of Germany.

These significant events culminated in the death of President Hindenburg on 2 August 1934. Hitler used this opportunity to merge the offices of chancellor and president, naming himself Führer, or supreme leader of Germany. The army and civil service swore a personal oath of allegiance to Adolf Hitler, giving him near total control of Germany.

6.1.2 Fear and state terrorism

Some historians argue that the Nazis were able to stay in power between 1933 and 1939 because they terrorised the German public into supporting them. For example, the historian T. Mergel argued that acts of terror were one aspect of the National Socialists' attempt to enforce their rule. This programme of terror was carried out by the SS, the use of political prisons and a powerful police force.

The SS and the concentration camps

The SS was set up in 1925 as an elite arm within the SA. By 1929, the group had come under the command of Heinrich Himmler, and by 1936 it had assumed control over all police and secret police functions. The SS was staffed by ambitious academics, civil servants and military officers. Himmler declared that the organisation was to form the new aristocratic elite in Germany, and potential applicants were screened for 'true Aryan lineage' to conform with Nazi racial ideology and mythology. However, the most important quality sought in SS members was total obedience to Hitler and the Nazi Party.

By 1934 the SS had become so important that it was now the primary agent of radicalisation in Germany. Through its leadership and with the support of Hitler, the SS gained extreme powers and operated outside the law.

One of the main purposes of the SS was to run the early political prisons. These were classified as 'concentration camps'. The first concentration camp was built in March 1933 at Dachau, in Bavaria. By the middle of 1933 nearly 30,000 political prisoners, mostly communists and social democrats, had been interned in Dachau. Subsequent camps were opened in Sachsenhausen and Buchenwald. It is important to note that these camps were not yet the death camps of **anti-Semitic** genocide. Still, inmates faced brutal treatment. They were dressed in military-style uniform and lived in harsh, unsanitary conditions. They were given work details outside the camps that involved long hours and backbreaking work.

The historian R. J. Evans describes the treatment prisoners endured (Source 1).

> ## SOURCE 1
>
> At least seventy camps had been hastily erected in the course of the seizure of power in the early months of 1933, alongside an unknown but probably even larger number of torture cellars and small prisons in the SA's various branches and headquarters. Around 45,000 prisoners were held in them at this time, beaten, tortured and ritually humiliated by their guards. Several hundred died as a result of their maltreatment. The vast majority were Communists, Social Democrats, and trade unionists.
>
> **Evans, R. J. (2006) *The Third Reich in Power*, Penguin**

The fear of arrest became a powerful tool in helping Hitler to maintain power. It allowed the Nazis to intimidate potential opposition. Communists and social democrats had been the fiercest critics of the Nazis, but imprisonment in the brutal prison camps acted as a strong deterrent, silencing the opposition. This played at least some role in helping Hitler to stay in power between 1933 and 1939.

The Gestapo, the police and the courts

The work of the police and the courts also proved a strong deterrent to opposition.

Perhaps the most feared organisation was the Gestapo, a political police force under the control of the SS, which within Hitler's regime had near unlimited powers. The Gestapo targeted potential opponents of the Nazis and was given free rein to investigate or detain suspects. There was no need for physical evidence and often they relied on hearsay provided by a network of undercover informers. Initially the Gestapo successfully infiltrated and arrested members of communist and social democrat groups, including workers. But by the late 1930s the organisation's role had moved on to advancing the Nazis' racial aims through the persecution of the Jews. So-called block wardens supported the work of the Gestapo. These were local Nazis who supervised neighbourhoods, monitoring the public for any sign of disquiet or disobedience against the Nazi regime.

Some historians have argued that the Gestapo was a highly professional corps, so effective that its members were able to detect any threat to Hitler's rule. As such, the Gestapo gave Hitler and the Nazis free rein when it came to suppressing opposition. Moreover, the secret nature of the operation of the police generated even greater fear and mistrust among ordinary Germans, further helping Hitler tighten his grip on power between 1933 and 1939.

While the terrifying effects of Gestapo surveillance in Nazi Germany are well known, in many ways the work of the regular courts and police force was just as important in enabling Hitler to retain power. Through the early decrees of 1933, opponents of the Nazis had been removed from civil service positions. These powers were further extended to the courts. In 1934, Hitler created the Volksgerichtshof, or People's Courts. These courts had a political directive to prosecute enemies of the state and they frequently prosecuted opponents of Nazism with little or no evidence.

The work of the courts and police force helped Hitler to stay in power as it further strengthened his ability to deter and remove opponents. He possessed total control over not only the secret police but also the regular tools of law and order, which made it near impossible to challenge him or his party.

On the other hand…

While it may appear that Hitler had near total control over the German legal system, there are limitations to the argument that this is what allowed him to stay in power. For example, most of the early concentration camps were forced to close in late 1933 and early 1934. A camp set up in Stettin, in modern-day Poland, was examined by a local state prosecutor, who determined that both its existence and those working in it were breaking the law. Not only was the camp shut down, but several SS officers were tried and given lengthy prison sentences.

Moreover, there were parts of Germany where the Gestapo exercised little practical control due to a lack of personnel. For example, in Düsseldorf, which had a population of over 4 million people, there were only 281 Gestapo officers. This limits the argument that the Gestapo was the main reason for Hitler's ability to maintain control of Germany between 1933 and 1939.

Overall

Nevertheless, there is compelling evidence to support the idea that Hitler and the Nazi Party were able to exercise significant control through fear. With total, or near total, control over the police and the courts, the secret informers of the Gestapo and the fear of being sent to a concentration camp, Hitler was able to eliminate the opposition and deter any future unrest. Everything that happened in Germany occurred in an atmosphere of fear and terror, enabling Hitler to maintain his iron grip on power.

6.1.3 Propaganda

It was not just terror and the threat of violence that enabled Hitler and the Nazis to maintain control of Germany. They also used a wide range of propaganda to 'sell' the idea of Nazism to the German public.

Joseph Goebbels, the Reich minister of propaganda, had control over the mass media, including the publication of books, newspapers and magazines, and the broadcast of radio programmes and films. Through this, he was able to advance Nazi ideologies, including the racial superiority of Aryan Germans as well as the 'Hitler Myth'. The myth claimed that Germany was beset by threats from Jewish people, communists and foreign states, and that Hitler was the only man who could save Germany from its enemies. Some historians argue that the use of propaganda increased support for Hitler and the Nazi Party, making it easier for them to stay in power between 1933 and 1939.

Mass media

Goebbels used all modern forms of media to communicate the Nazis' message to Germans. He explained the aim of this propaganda (Source 2).

> **SOURCE 2**
>
> 'It is not enough for people to be more or less reconciled to our regime, to be persuaded to adopt a neutral attitude towards us; rather we want to work on people until they have capitulated to us, until they grasp ideologically that what is happening in Germany today not only must be accepted but also can be accepted.'
>
> **Goebbels quoted in Noakes, J. and Pridham, G. (1988)** *Nazism 1919–1945. Volume 3: Foreign policy, War and Racial Extermination: A Documentary Reader*, **University of Exeter Press**

Figure 6.2 Goebbels in Berlin in 1934. He devised the use of the 'Hitler greeting', seen in this photo. This Nazi salute was designed to boost support for and identification with the Nazi regime

One way he was able to achieve this was through the mass media. For example, the Reich Press Law of 1933 purged newspapers of left-wing, Jewish and liberal editors. A Reich Association of German Newspapers was set up, and all journalists were required to join. This meant the Nazis could prevent opposition journalists from producing work. The Nazis also published their own paper, the *Völkischer Beobachter* ('Racial Observer'), which had a daily circulation of over 120,000 copies in 1931 and over a million by 1941.

All of these factors enabled the Nazis to dominate the popular newspaper market. They promoted pro-Nazi stories, removed opposition journalists and effectively stifled freedom of speech. This arguably played a major role in helping Hitler maintain control of Germany between 1933 and 1939.

Another tool that the Nazis used to spread their ideas was the radio. Goebbels quickly realised the potential of radio. He stated that 'What the press was in the nineteenth century, radio will be for the twentieth century.' At Goebbels' request, an engineer developed radio receivers which were very cheap to purchase or could be hired at a low monthly cost. The new 'people's receivers', as they came to be known, made the new radio technology accessible to the general public, and by 1939, 70 per cent of households owned a radio. They were also common in workplaces, schools and even public streets. The radios were designed to be short range, so that they picked up Nazi-controlled channels only, meaning Hitler's speeches, Nazi ideas and propaganda were broadcast straight into millions of homes across Germany.

As Goebbels' propaganda machine grew in both power and reach, the day-to-day lives of millions of Germans became saturated with the Nazi propaganda message. Arguably, this was a major factor in achieving Goebbels' main aim – to encourage millions of Germans to accept the ideals of the Nazi Party.

To achieve his goals, Goebbels also took control of the German film industry, and in doing so removed Jewish and left-wing producers, actors and directors. These included actors like Marlene Dietrich, who emigrated to the USA and became a famous Hollywood actor. Goebbels, himself trained and experienced in film, wanted to prioritise escapist films that he believed would be popular among the general public. However, he was partially overruled by Hitler, who wanted cinema to advance the idea of a racially pure Germany. This led to the making of films such as 1940's *Der ewige Jude* (*The Eternal Jew*), an anti-Semitic propaganda piece presented as a documentary, and *Ich klage an* (*I Accuse*), a pro-**euthanasia** propaganda piece.

Figure 6.3 A film poster advertising *Der ewige Jude* (*The Eternal Jew*). Anti-Semitic films like this were Hitler's idea, although the German public were often reluctant to attend screenings of films that they saw as little more than propaganda

Hitler's control of the German film industry arguably helped him to maintain power as he was able to further influence German popular culture by weaving Nazi ideology into the art of film. In this way, Nazi ideas reached a larger audience, which helped build support for the regime between 1933 and 1939.

Rallies

As well as making use of the mass media, Hitler and the Nazis were arguably able to generate support for their regime through popular and dramatic rallies. These helped Nazism not only to appear to have popular support but also somehow to be ancient and established. The rallies usually involved speeches, mass marches, flags, spotlights and torches. They were expertly choreographed and designed to build suspense and excitement. They were so powerful, the American journalist W. Shirer declared, 'I'm beginning to comprehend, I think, some of the reasons for Hitler's astonishing success.' The rallies gave the impression of strength, discipline and unity, all of which were a powerful contrast to the seemingly fragmented period of Weimar Germany.

Mass rallies helped Hitler to stay in power as through them the Nazi Party appeared not only popular but hugely successful, which won over millions of cynics. The idea of a strong, disciplined leadership was very appealing to many ordinary Germans, especially given the context of the challenges Germany had faced in the 1920s.

On the other hand...

One could argue that Nazi propaganda is not the main reason why Hitler was able to stay in power between 1933 and 1939. For one, realistically the Nazis struggled to control the output of every single newspaper in the country. Indeed, by the end of 1939 there were over a thousand newspapers in circulation in Germany, and the Nazis were only able to control an estimated 70 per cent of these.

Moreover, Hitler's strategy of producing overtly propagandist films appeared to backfire. In fact, attendance dropped when propaganda films were screened.

As the historian S. Lee argues (Source 3):

SOURCE 3

The result [of Nazi control of media] was a bland form of journalism which produced a decline in public interest. Throughout the period, the regime was never able to use the press to generate support.

Lee, S. (2010) *Hitler and Nazi Germany* **(2nd edn), Routledge**

Overall

It is clear to see that much debate surrounds the influence of propaganda in helping Hitler retain power between 1933 and 1939. While the Nazis exercised a great deal of control over the mass media, the impact this had on the general public is difficult to measure. Rallies and events were evidently well attended, but propaganda films grew increasingly less popular. However, it does seem fair to argue that propaganda played an important role in perpetuating the Nazi regime during this period.

6.1.4 Economic policies

Another way in which Hitler tried to win favour with the German public was by appearing to make drastic improvements to the economy. Through the planning of the Reich minister of economics, Hjalmar Schacht, and the introduction of the so-called Four-Year Plan in 1936, it seemed that the Nazis were able to make rapid improvements to the economy they inherited in 1933. These economic improvements may have convinced Germans to support Hitler, therefore making it easier for him to stay in power.

Schacht and Nazi economic policy

Hjalmar Schacht was a gifted economist with many years' experience of working in government. He had been involved in fixing hyperinflation in 1923 and was strongly opposed to what he saw as unjust reparation payments. He oversaw economic planning for much of the period between 1933 and 1937. His economic policy called for high levels of government spending and a significant level of state involvement in the economy. For example, government spending as a percentage of GDP was 17.9 per cent in 1932 and rose to 33.5 per cent in 1938. This caused a large growth in the German economy, enabling it to overtake the size of the pre-Depression economy by the mid-1930s. Levels of production also grew, sparked by programmes of rearmament and investment in public works. Between 1929 and 1939 there was over a tenfold increase in production in Germany, and unemployment fell sharply. By 1935 unemployment had fallen to 1.7 million and it was nearly eliminated by 1939. This seemed a particularly dramatic improvement given that at the height of the Depression unemployment stood at nearly 6 million.

Figure 6.4 A new German motorway, or autobahn, in the late 1930s. Public works like these helped boost the economy, as well as improve infrastructure

Some historians argue that these economic improvements helped Hitler stay in power between 1933 and 1939. Given the hardships many Germans endured in the 1920s and early 1930s, such stability would have been a powerful influence on people's support, or at least tolerance, of Nazi rule, since it brought such economic rewards.

Farmers

It was not only the industrial and urban economy that appeared to grow in this period in Germany, as the Nazi Party also took steps to invest in the rural economy. This arguably secured support from farmers and agricultural workers, helping the Nazis stay in power.

As well as the so-called Great Depression, there had been an agricultural depression in Germany in the 1920s and early 1930s. Measures were introduced by the Reich minister of agriculture, Alfred Hugenberg, to improve the conditions for farmers. He cancelled debts and paid out 650 million Reichsmarks to peasant farmers and estate managers to ensure their farms were financially secure. This was significantly higher than the 454 million Reichsmarks paid out by the Weimar government between 1926 and 1933. Many farmers were also protected from losing their farms if they failed to repay debts. Overall, farmers' wages increased by 41 per cent between 1933 and 1938, a greater increase than among the urban working class.

This made it easier for Hitler to stay in power, as it not only secured food production but helped retain the loyalty of rural and agricultural workers.

Worker policies and 'benefits'

As well as economic improvements, the Nazis aimed to introduce schemes to improve the quality of life for many Germans. They did this through schemes such as Strength Through Joy (KdF) and the German Labour Front (DAF).

The improvements these schemes made are highlighted by the historian J. Caplan (Source 4).

SOURCE 4

Other arms of the Nazi [state] took over labour, welfare, sports and organized leisure, and managed occupational and social groups from teachers and doctors to veterans and women. The Deutsche Arbeitsfront (DAF), the mass-membership labour organization led by the erratic Robert Ley and charged with the crucial task of controlling the working class, employed 44,000 paid and 1.3 million unpaid officials. Its most popular sections, Beauty of Labour (SdA) and Strength Through Joy (KdF) provided workplace amenities, organized leisure, and subsidized holidays for the masses; it organized the travel of 10,000 football fans to London for a December friendly at White Hart Lane, and built a 'KdF town' in Berlin to receive German visitors to the 1936 Olympics.

Caplan, J. (2019) *Nazi Germany: A Very Short Introduction*, Oxford University Press

---

These benefits schemes, which provided economic, social and welfare incentives to a previously overlooked population, helped Hitler to gain the support of a potentially hostile working class, making it easier for him to stay in power from 1933 to 1939.

On the other hand...

It is worth noting that by 1932 the global economy was slowly recovering, boosting levels of international demand and production and helping to grow the German economy. When Hitler became chancellor in 1933 he was able to falsely take credit for improving the economic situation. Therefore, it was economic factors outside of Hitler's control, rather than Hitler himself, that enabled him to stay in power in this period.

Moreover, although the economy did seem to be recovering, there is much debate about the degree to which this actually improved the lives of ordinary Germans. When we take a closer look at wages during this period, it becomes clear that the economic situation of working-class earners did not improve significantly between 1933 and 1939. Hourly wages in 1933 were 97 per cent of 1932 levels, and this had only increased to 98 per cent by 1939. This limits the argument that it was economic improvements that helped Hitler to retain power between 1933 and 1939.

Moreover, there is evidence that not all farmers supported Nazi agrarian policies. The historian R. J. Evans highlights this point (Source 5).

SOURCE 5

By the summer of 1934 peasant farmers had turned against the Nazis' agrarian policies everywhere; in Bavaria the atmosphere on market-days was said to be so hostile to the [Nazi] Party that local [Nazi officials] did not dare intervene, and well-known Nazis avoided the farmers for fear they would be subjected to a barrage of aggressive questions. Even in areas like Schleswig-Holstein, where the rural population had voted in overwhelming numbers for the Nazi Party in 1930–33, the peasants were said by July 1934 to be depressed, particularly about the price they were getting for their pigs.

Evans, R. J. (2006) *The Third Reich in Power*, **Penguin**

Overall

It seems clear that there was, to one degree or another, economic improvement in Germany between 1933 and 1939. Production increased, farmers were protected from **foreclosure**, unemployment was reduced and improvements were made to infrastructure. Although Hitler and the Nazi Party never achieved the full economic independence they strove for, the economy in 1939 appeared stronger than it had in 1933. Comparatively, it also seemed that Germany had been more successful than other countries in recovering from the Great Depression. Indeed, while Germany had reduced unemployment to 300,000 by 1939, Britain still had 1.8 million unemployed workers at that time. This clearly played a significant role in helping Hitler retain the support of ordinary workers, farmers, the middle class and businessmen, which made it much easier for the Nazis to remain in power.

6.1.5 Social policies

Another way Hitler and the Nazi Party were able to maintain power was to create the concept of a new, ideal society. This so-called **Volksgemeinschaft** would be racially pure and remove groups of people whom the Nazis regarded as 'undesirable', such as Jewish, Slavic and disabled people. This would enable Hitler to build an 'Aryan' society that would hold traditional values and social structures. Despite the fact that by 1939 only 10 per cent of Germans were active members of the Nazi Party, through these policies Hitler aimed to influence all of society and create a community in which Germans felt a sense of belonging. There is an argument that the creation of this Volksgemeinschaft through a variety of social policies made it easier for Hitler to control German society, therefore enabling him to stay in power from 1933 to 1939.

Youth and education policies

One way the Nazis controlled society was through education policy. First, the Nazis aimed to control teachers and education officials. As we have seen, by 1933, it was mandatory for civil servants to join the Nazi Party. However, by 1936, 36 per cent of teachers had also joined the party – a higher number than in many other professions. The Nazis created the National Socialist Teachers' League (NS-Lehrerbund), which replaced other teaching groups, and by 1937 nearly all teachers belonged to this group and the majority accepted the need to ideologically educate schoolchildren.

The school curriculum also changed dramatically. Jewish students were first limited in number, and by 1938 excluded totally from schools. Students began their lessons with a 'Hitler greeting', and Nazi propaganda and youth groups were a part of daily school life. Schools placed emphasis on subjects like PE, which, at five hours at least per week, was compulsory. The teaching of many other subjects was altered drastically, too. Biology was used to claim that there was a significant difference between various races, and history was used to glorify old German myths, as well as teach about recent 'injustices' such as the Treaty of Versailles.

These changes allowed Hitler to gain control of society, as he was able to **indoctrinate** Germans from a very young age. With a constant barrage of Nazi messaging, children would have found it hard to resist the Nazi ideology, either actively or passively. This meant that many young Germans accepted Hitler's rule without question, making it much easier for Hitler to stay in power between 1933 and 1939.

Figure 6.5 Scenes like this one from a German school in 1934 were common. The Nazis created an education system that was designed to brainwash young people into supporting or, at the very least, accepting Nazi rule

Nazi control of young Germans was further extended via youth groups. These groups taught young Germans about their role in society and built upon the lessons that children received in school. Between the ages of six and ten, children joined the Pimpfen, or Little Fellows. Those aged 10 to 14 joined the Deutsches Jungvolk, or German Young People. At 14 this group was split into boys, who joined the Hitlerjugend, or Hitler Youth, and girls, who joined the Bund Deutscher Mädel, the League of German Girls, or Maidens. Boys focused on military-style subjects and girls more domestic ones. By 1936, all non-Nazi youth groups had been banned, and by 1939, membership of a Nazi youth group was compulsory.

These groups aimed to indoctrinate young Germans into possessing an unquestioning loyalty towards the Nazi regime and accepting the spirit of the new Volksgemeinschaft. This engendered growing acceptance to Hitler's regime, making it significantly easier for him to retain control of Germany from 1933 to 1939.

Churches

Hitler was also aiming to win the cooperation of the Protestant Church and the Catholic Church. He insisted on church reform, to ensure they conformed to the new Nazi society, and this was broadly accepted by German religious leaders. Hitler was fiercely anti-Semitic and anti-communist, and both of these policies appealed to many members of the socially conservative German churches.

In 1933, a Reich Church (the German Evangelical Church) was formed, a successor to the pre-existing German Protestant Church. It was led by a Reich bishop and members referred to themselves as German Christians. Nazi flags and uniforms were integrated into services and the German swastika replaced the Christian cross. Then, in July, Hitler reached a **concordat** with the **Pope**. This guaranteed that the Pope would not interfere in Hitler's control of Germany, provided Hitler did not interfere with the business of the Catholic Church. Though Hitler ultimately reneged on this promise, it guaranteed that he would not be challenged by the Pope.

This made it easier to control Germany as German Christians were arguably more likely to support Hitler and the Nazis. This support played a significant role in Hitler's ability to retain power between 1933 and 1939.

Women

Women were to play a key role in the new Volksgemeinschaft, as mothers for the Reich. They were expected to reject modern fashions, such as wearing make-up, stop smoking (there were reports of SA patrols physically stopping women smoking in public), and become as fit and healthy as possible in order to bear the next Aryan generation. Women were expected not to work or pursue further education, but rather to focus on a domestic life of *Kinder, Küche, Kirche* (children, the kitchen and the church). Women were intended to represent a new feminine ideal. Girls were encouraged to wear traditional dress and have their hair in pigtails.

The Nazis took further measures to increase the birth rate. Abortion was prohibited, contraception was limited, and financial rewards were given to those parents who bore several children. Mothers were awarded a medal, the Mother's Cross of Honour, which was designed to encourage large families.

This aided Hitler's control of Germany as he was able to encourage greater social control over women and families. This insistence on conformity to the ideals of the Volksgemeinschaft allowed Hitler to engineer the types of family and gender roles he felt were necessary to advancing Germany's interests.

Figure 6.6 The Mother's Cross of Honour medal was introduced by decree in December 1938 and was awarded to women who had conceived and raised at least four children

On the other hand…

Although most teachers and educational resources were influenced by Nazi ideas, not all were. While the Nazis controlled the production of new educational materials, there is some evidence that when certain books were produced, they included some ideologically focused sections, and then other, more general ones. This gave teachers scope to deliver fewer indoctrinating lessons.

Moreover, while many German Christians supported the Nazi regime, some did not. Some Protestant ministers even formed the Confessional Church. Led by Martin Niemöller and Dietrich Bonhoeffer, the church rejected the role of the Nazi state in religion. Many of these ministers were arrested, including Niemöller himself. By the late 1930s individual Catholic priests were resisting Nazi rule, such as in Oldenburg, where Nazi officials had removed crucifixes from classrooms.

Also, although it was planned for women to remain in domestic life, this did not materialise. Indeed, by the late 1930s Germany had one of the highest proportions of women employed in the workforce.

Overall

It is very hard to measure how much individual Germans supported the idea of the Volksgemeinschaft. While it is true that membership of the Nazi Party remained low, wholesale curricular reform, influence over teachers and compulsory membership of youth groups all engendered a sense of Nazism's control over young people. The opportunities for women were significantly reduced, and girls' early years were geared to preparing them for domestic family life. It even appeared as if the overwhelming majority of German churches supported Hitler's desire for a socially conservative

Germany. Taken together, this would have been a powerful influence over the day-to-day life of ordinary Germans. Moreover, given the Nazi drive to remove people they characterised as 'asocial', such as Jewish, homosexual and Romani people and those with disabilities, from the Volksgemeinschaft, this would have been further encouragement to Germans to accept social control through fear of being violently excluded from society. This certainly played a role in helping Hitler to stay in power from 1933 to 1939.

How did Hitler stay in power?

It is clear that there were several factors behind Hitler's ability to stay in power between 1933 and 1939. The totalitarian nature of his rule gave him huge powers over the German population. His use of terror and violence further discouraged any potential opposition to his regime. The camps became a powerful symbol of the fate of those who stood up to Hitler. However, it was not only threats and legal controls that allowed Hitler to control Germany. The Nazis provided encouragements to 'deserving' members of the Volksgemeinschaft through social and economic policies, as well as trying to engender a sense of allegiance to the regime via propaganda, education, the Volksgemeinschaft and rallies.

The discussion in this chapter should allow you to evaluate the importance of each of these factors and craft an argument about which of these was the most important in allowing Hitler to stay in power between 1933 and 1939.

ACTIVITIES

1 Create a mind map:
   a) Place 'How could Hitler stay in power?' in the centre.
   b) Write three stems – social, economic and political.
   c) Find as many facts for each stem as you can.
   d) Annotate the mind map. Try to include one small drawing per fact. This will aid your memory.

2 Create a list of all examples of fear that Hitler used to control Germany.
   a) Prioritise these in order of effectiveness, numbering them from 1 = most effective, down to the least effective.
   b) Justify why you have selected your number 1.

3 Create a list of the propaganda methods that Hitler and Goebbels used to control Germany.
   a) Prioritise these in order of effectiveness, numbering them from 1 = most effective, down to the least effective.
   b) Justify why you have selected your number 1.

4 Create an argument.
   a) What do you think was the most important reason behind Hitler's ability to stay in power?
   b) Find three pieces of evidence that support your argument. Try to develop each with an example.
   c) Explain how each piece of evidence supports your argument.
   d) Explain why the factor you have picked is more important than any other factor.

GLOSSARY

Term	Meaning
anti-Semitic	Hostile to or prejudiced against Jewish people.
authoritarian	Favouring or enforcing strict obedience to authority at the expense of personal freedom.
concordat	An agreement or treaty, especially one between the Vatican and a secular government relating to matters of mutual interest.
euthanasia	The act of deliberately ending someone's life to relieve perceived or real suffering, used by the Nazis to justify the systematic murder of, initially, people with disabilities.
fascism	An authoritarian and nationalistic right-wing system of government and social organisation.
foreclosure	When property is seized by a bank after loan payments have been missed.
GDP	The total value of goods produced and services provided in a country during a single year.
Gleichschaltung	The standardisation of political, economic and social institutions as carried out in authoritarian states.
indoctrinate	Teach a person or group to accept a set of beliefs uncritically.
Pope	The Bishop of Rome as head of the Roman Catholic Church.
propaganda	Information, especially of a biased or misleading nature, used to promote a political cause or point of view.
public works	The work of building such infrastructure as roads, schools and hospitals, carried out by the state for the community.
Reich	The German state.
Reichsrat	A senate-style assembly in which each region had equal representation during the period of the Weimar Republic.
Schutzstaffel (SS)	Initially formed to provide security for Hitler and Nazi Party officials, the SS quickly expanded to perform a variety of political, security and military functions.
Sturmabteilung (SA)	The Nazi Party's paramilitary wing.
totalitarianism	A system of government that is centralised and dictatorial and requires complete subservience to the state.
Volksgemeinschaft	A racially unified society made up of people of one 'Volk', or nation.

Index

Acknowledgements

Photo credits

Photos reproduced by permission of: **pp.vi, 18 & 21** © SZ Photo/Sammlung Megele/Bridgeman Images; **pp.1** and **10** © Niday Picture Library/Alamy Stock Photo; **p.2** © Robert Alfers, kgberger via Wikipedia/https:// creativecommons.org/licenses/by-sa/3.0/; **p.5** © Leemage/Universal Images Group via Getty Images; **p.6** © Harry Hampel/ullstein bild via Getty Images; **p.12** © Bridgeman Images; **p.23** © Pictorial Press Ltd/Alamy Stock Photo; **p.28** © Heritage Image Partnership Ltd/Alamy Stock Photo; **p.30** © History and Art Collection/Alamy Stock Photo; **pp.35 & 37** © The Picture Art Collection/Alamy Stock Photo; **p.38** © Lebrecht Music & Arts/Alamy Stock Photo; **p.41** © Ws-KuLa via Wikipedia (https://creativecommons.org/licenses/by-sa/3.0/); p.44 © Meyers Konversationslexikon, 5th edition/Angr/Public Domain; **pp.48 & 56** © The Picture Art Collection/Alamy Stock Photo; **p.49** © IanDagnall Computing/Alamy Stock Photo; **p.51** © Armémuseum (The Swedish Army Museum)/ Public Domain; **p.52** © Historic Collection/Alamy Stock Photo; **p.55** © Universal History Archive/Getty Images; **p.60** © akg-images; **pp.64 & 77** © Suddeutsche Zeitung Photo/Alamy Stock Photo; **p.67** © Sueddeutsche Zeitung Photo/Alamy Stock Photo; **p.71** © INTERFOTO/Alamy Stock Photo; **p.73** © Granger Historical Picture Archive/ Alamy Stock Photo; **p.75** © INTERFOTO/Alamy Stock Photo; **p.79** © INTERFOTO/Alamy Stock Photo; **pp.83 & 96** © Suddeutsche Zeitung Photo/Alamy Stock Photo; **p.86** © Suddeutsche Zeitung Photo/Alamy Stock Photo; **p.90** © Everett Collection Inc/Alamy Stock Photo; **p.91** © World History Archive/Alamy Stock Photo; **p.93** © World History Archive/Alamy Stock Photo; **p.98** © Stephen French/Alamy Stock Photo.

Text credits

pp.3 & 13 extracts from *Germany from Napoleon to Bismarck: 1800–1866* by Thomas Nipperdey, translated by Daniel Nolan. Copyright © 1996. Republished with permission of Princeton University Press. Permission conveyed through Copyright Clearance Center, Inc.; **pp.4, 5, 13, 26, 32, 39, 54, 55 & 61** nine extracts from *A Concise History of Germany* (3rd edition) by Mary Fulbrook, published by Cambridge University Press. Copyright © Mary Fulbrook 2019. Reproduced with permission of Cambridge University Press through PLSclear; **pp.8 & 20** two extracts from 'The Formation of German Nationalism, 1740–1850', by Christian Jansen in H. W. Smith (ed.) *The Oxford Handbook of Modern German History*. Copyright © Christian Jansen 2011, 2015. Reproduced with permission of Oxford University Press through PLSclear; **pp.9 & 22** extracts from *The History of Germany Since 1789* by Golo Mann, translated by Marian Jackson and published by Praeger, 1968; **p.19** extract from *The Oxford Handbook of Modern German History* by Helmut Walser Smith. Copyright © Helmut Walser Smith 2011, 2015. Reproduced with permission of Oxford University Press through PLSclear; **pp.22, 24, 40 & 53** four extracts from *Access to History: The Unification of Germany and the Challenge of Nationalism 1789–1919* by Alan Farmer. Copyright © Alan Farmer 2020. Reproduced by permission of Hodder Education; **p.31** extract from *The Ascendancy of Europe 1815–1914* by Anderson, M. S. Copyright © 2014 Anderson, M. S. Reproduced by permission of Taylor and Francis Group, LLC, a division of Informa plc.; **p.43** extract from *German Nationalism and Religious Conflict: Culture, Ideology, Politics 1870–1914* by Helmut Walser Smith. Copyright © 1995. Republished with permission of Princeton University Press. Permission conveyed through Copyright Clearance Center, Inc.; **p.44** extract from *Religion im Umbruch Deutschland 1870–1918* by Thomas Nipperdey, published by C. H. Beck, 1988; **p.48** extract from *Bismarck and the German Empire, 1871–1918* by Lynn Abrams. Copyright © 1995 Lynn Abrams. Reproduced by permission of Taylor and Francis Group, LLC, a division of Informa plc.; **p.57** extract from Bismarck's 'Blood and Iron' speech (1862). Translated in *Bismarck and Europe* by Medlicott, W. N. and Coveney, D. K. and published by St Martin's Press, 1971; **p.66** extract from *The Weimar Republic: Overture to the Third Reich* by Godfrey Scheele, published by Faber & Faber, 1946; **pp.66 & 69** two extracts from *The Coming of the Third Reich: How the Nazis Destroyed Democracy and Seized Power in Germany* by Richard J. Evans. Copyright © Richard J. Evans 2003. Published by Penguin Books 2004. Reprinted by permission of Penguin Books Limited; **p.70** transcript adapted from the National Archives website: www.nationalarchives.gov.uk/education/greatwar/transcript/g5cs1s3t.htm. Contains public sector information licensed under the Open Government Licence v3.0 (www.nationalarchives.gov. uk/doc/open-government-licence/version/3/); **p.72** extracts from *The Weimar Republic* by Stephen Lee. Copyright © 2010 Stephen Lee. Reproduced by permission of Taylor and Francis Group, LLC, a division of Informa plc.;

p.76 extract from *From Weimar to Auschwitz* by Hans Mommsen, translated by Philip O'Connor and published by Princeton University Press, 1991; **pp.78 & 94** two extracts from *Nazi Germany: A Very Short Introduction* by Jane Caplan. Copyright © Jane Caplan 2019. Reproduced with permission of Oxford University Press through PLSclear; **pp.88 & 95** two extracts from *The Third Reich in Power* by Richard J. Evans. Copyright © Richard J. Evans 2005. Published by Allen Lane 2005, Penguin Books 2006. Reprinted by permission of Penguin Books Limited; **p.89** extract from *Nazism 1919–1945. Volume 3: Foreign Policy, War and Racial Extermination: A Documentary Reader* by Jeremy Noakes and Geoffrey Pridham. Published by University of Exeter Press 1988. Reproduced with permission of University of Exeter Press through PLSclear; **p.92** extract from *The Rise and Fall of the Third Reich: A History of Nazi Germany* by William L. Shirer, published by Simon & Schuster, 1960; **p.92** extract from *Hitler and Nazi Germany* (2nd edition) by Stephen Lee. Copyright © 2010 Stephen Lee. Reproduced by permission of Taylor and Francis Group, LLC, a division of Informa plc.